Go
Slow
Now:
Faulkner
and the
Race
Question

Faulkner
and the
Race
Question

BY

CHARLES D. PEAVY

University of Oregon Books • EUGENE, OREGON

Foreword

As the author of *Go Slow Now* admits promptly in his own "Introduction," William Faulkner's interest in the American Negro has not escaped the attention of a wide variety of scholars, critics, reporters, and assorted other writers who have recorded a spectrum of opinions ranging from high praise to bitter adverse criticism. The existence of most of these many reactions is acknowledged appropriately in the pages and footnotes of *Go Slow Now*.

The most important justification of Charles D. Peavy's essay is his attempt to bring together and to focus upon practically everything Faulkner had to say on the subject of the Negro, whether in his fiction or in a considerable body of articles, letters, and other scattered sources. Without excessive attempt at critical debate, the author sets out to examine what Faulkner actually said and to determine the meaning of what he said, without the exercise of preconceived notions.

It must be remembered that the Faulkner who has been rightly acclaimed as one of the major literary creators of the present century was also a man who not only inherited a tradition but who lived, suffered, and achieved during a recent period which demanded serious and dramatic questioning of that tradition, along with several others—a process which continues after Faulkner's death. Therefore, Faulkner's own views cannot be expected to have remained static, and since the artist who produced the fiction was also a human being, both his fiction and his expository writings of all sorts must be considered if a given view is to be attributed to him as characteristic of his thought, particularly about the Negro.

Among the positive merits of the present study is the simple fact that there is abundant evidence that the writer has read Faulkner more carefully than seems to be the fashion in a surprising number of the ever-increasing flood of articles and books which constitute continuing Faulkner scholarship and commentary. Perhaps no modern writer has been more frequently and carelessly misquoted than Faulkner, not infrequently at the expense of the meaning of the passage quoted. Peavy's pages which follow reveal the care which has been exerted to avoid that particular pitfall.

In addition, the author—as chance would have it—has had a more sustained opportunity to observe people, places, events, and situations more closely akin (despite the passage of time) to those of Faulkner's actual and fictional worlds than have some of the scholars who seem to have thought that a week or so in Oxford, Mississippi, would provide an adequate knowledge of the atmosphere of Faulkner's Jefferson and its environs. Such a more sensitive awareness of important elements of Faulkner's own heritage reveals itself in the analysis of the evidence presented at a number of points in *Go Slow Now*.

That Professor Peavy's essay is the result of mature deliberation is also evidenced by the respectable number of articles which have appeared over his name in several scholarly journals. Whether or not references to all of these pieces are to be found at appropriate points in the following pages, the reader with a detailed awareness of the extensive bibliography of Faulkner criticism will be reassured that Peavy has already served his apprenticeship in Faulkner studies. Here, whether the informed reader tends to agree or disagree with conclusions stated or suggested, a serious weighing and evaluating of the evidence presented is, in effect, demanded. It should also be remarked that even the more general, or casual, reader of Faulkner should be able to derive from these pages useful insights either for reflection upon what has already been read —especially the stories and the novels—or as a stimulus for additional reading.

Yet another importance of *Go Slow Now* is the thoroughness with which new or relatively fugitive materials drawn from Faulkner's nonfictional writing are presented. These materials range from "public utterances," to correspondence (including letters published in newspapers and magazines), to records of interviews. Isolated testimony drawn from such sources easily leads to a misunderstanding, even a misrepresentation, of Faulkner. One of Peavy's purposes is to organize the testimony in such a way as to avoid misrepresentation and in order to decrease the possibility of misunderstanding whenever possible. He is, however, careful not to project for Faulkner the development of a systematic philosophy on the subject of the Negro, whether represented fictionally or as the principal protagonist in civil rights controversies. Faulkner died without finding simple solutions to the many attendant problems, but the totality of his work is graphic evidence of an articulate deep and abiding concern with such problems, a concern more accurately reflecting the dilemma of an entire region than the reams of polemic printed materials which have ignored the paradoxes Faulkner thought he saw engendered between truth and fact. For those who genuinely wish to understand Faulkner's views, the pages of *Go Slow Now* should be enlightening.

PATRICK G. HOGAN, JR.

FOR MY MOTHER

Acknowledgments

I have indicated my debt to published scholarship in the footnotes to the text of my discussion. There are other obligations, however, which I want to acknowledge separately. I am indebted to the National Endowment for the Arts and Humanities for a grant which allowed the research for this project to begin, and to the American Philosophical Society for a grant from the Penrose Fund for research in progress. I owe special thanks to Mrs. John Faulkner for imparting to me personal information concerning Faulkner's disagreement with his brother John on the race issue, and to Russell Warren Howe for graciously supplying me with information concerning his interview with Faulkner on the race question. Thanks are also due Horace Judson, who gave me further facts about the Howe interview. I am obliged to Miss Zelda Osborne of the University of Houston Libraries for her unfailing assistance in obtaining necessary documents at short notice. My debts to Professor Sylvan Karchmer are many, but for his encouragement and assistance in the final stages of my project I am deeply grateful. I am also grateful to my colleague Patrick G. Hogan who gave me much valuable advice during the preparation of the first and second drafts of the manuscript and who also assisted in the task of proofreading. Acknowledgments are made to Random House for permission to quote from the following works by Faulkner: *Absalom, Absalom!*, *Collected Stories*, *Go Down Moses*, *The Hamlet*, *Intruder in the Dust*, *Light in August*, *The*

Unvanquished. Acknowledgments are made to Dodd, Mead, and Company for permission to quote Paul Laurence Dunbar's poem "We Wear the Mask." Acknowledgments are made to the University of Virginia Press for permission to quote from *Faulkner in the University* and to *Ebony* magazine to quote from Faulkner's "If I Were a Negro." Thanks are due to the *CLA Journal* for permission to quote from my article "Faulkner and the Howe Interview." I am particularly indebted to the University of Houston for a research grant which allowed me time from my teaching and other duties at the university to complete the manuscript. To Mrs. Catherine Lauris, Editor of University of Oregon Books, I express my appreciation for her valuable assistance in preparing the manuscript for publication. Finally, I acknowledge with affection the assistance of my wife, Professor Elysee H. Peavy, who aided me in the proofreading of the manuscript, galley, and page proof, and who assisted me in the preparation of the index.

C. D. P.

Introduction

The significance of Negro characters in the fiction of William Faulkner has long been noted. No other writer has been so fascinated with the American Negro, none has been so faithful in capturing the nuances of Negro speech and in delineating the characteristics of the race, and none has been as concerned with the plight of the Negro as a victimized member of society. Faulkner's almost obsessive interest in the Negro has, of course prompted a body of criticism which attempts to analyze his attitudes toward the Negro. Much of this literature is of the subjective or impressionistic variety, and unfortunately, much of it is quite erroneous. Some of the most blatant examples of critical misinterpretation are those advanced by Maxwell Geismar[1] and Charles I. Glicksberg,[2] who conclude that Faulkner fears and hates the Negro and, as a consequence, treats the Negro with contempt in his fiction. Geismar describes Faulkner as an unreconstructed rebel who expresses his great hatred of the entire complex of modern northern industrial society best in the "emancipated negro who to the Southern writer is the cause of the destruction of all he held dear."[3] The interpretations of Geismar and Glicksberg may be dismissed as prejudiced mis-

---

1 "William Faulkner: The Negro and the Female," *Writers in Crisis: The American Novel, 1925-1940* (Boston, 1942), pp. 141-183.
2 "William Faulkner and the Negro Problem," *Phylon* 10 (2nd Quarter, 1949), 157.
3 *Writers in Crisis*, p. 179.

readings of the text, but even such perceptive critics as Irving Howe and Robert Penn Warren have seen some of Faulkner's characters as an attempt to portray the Negro as ridiculous. At the other extreme is the view of Granville Hicks, that Faulkner is "one of the greatest friends of the Negro people because he wrote of them as people he not only loved but, more importantly, respected."[4] Still other critics have seen Faulkner as a Southern apologist for the *status quo,* or as one who looks back nostalgically on the plantation tradition and the paternalistic attitude toward Negroes. Most critics, however, have concluded that Faulkner has managed to overcome the racial prejudice of his region and has not only recognized the humanity of Negroes but has also often used them in his fiction to portray universal as well as racial problems. Notable among these critics are Dorothy D. Greer, Charles H. Nilon, Harvey Breit, Robert Bunker, Horace Gregory, and Ward L. Miner (for a complete listing of the investigators of Faulkner's attitudes toward the Negro, see the bibliography).

A smaller body of critics has attempted to ascertain precisely what attitudes Faulkner has toward equality, desegregation, and civil rights—a difficult task, at best, and one inevitably doomed to failure if limited solely to an examination of his works of fiction. Because Faulkner is an artist rather than a sociologist or political scientist, his work should not be expected to yield a systematic program for carrying out desegregation or implementing civil rights. As Irving Howe regretfully notes, one searches Faulkner's work in vain for any "strictly formulated political position on the Negro question" or any "clear and definite platform or coherent sociology" leading to the improvement of race relations,[5] yet many critics persist in deducing what they believe to be Faulkner's solution to the "Negro problem" from his fictional treatment of Negroes. This was certainly the case when the mounting tensions occasioned by Southern opposition to civil rights legislation caused Faulkner to mix polemics with fiction in *Intruder in the Dust,* a book which is part novel and part tract (Geismar, of course, saw this

---

[4] "Faulkner and His Town," *The Saturday Review* 48 (Oct. 2, 1965), 37.
[5] *William Faulkner, A Critical Study* (New York, 1952), p. 134.

novel as a "distorted but none the less sentimental and romantic expression of a familiar Southern chauvinism").[6] By 1950,
however, the opposition to the civil rights program was threatening to become violent, and Faulkner felt compelled to assume
the role of spokesman for the South in the mounting dissension
between what he felt to be two extremes. Faulkner began expressing his views on desegregation, equality, and civil rights
in a series of speeches, essays, and letters to the editors of
newspapers and magazines. A few critics, in attempting to
analyze Faulkner's views on race, have noted one or two of
these statements, but none has made a comprehensive assess-
ment of all his nonfiction statements. Some of Faulkner's
statements are ambivalent or contradictory, and many are controversial, particularly when they are viewed outside their
original context. As a result, Faulkner's views on race (both in
his fiction and his nonfiction) have been attacked by liberals
and conservatives alike. He has been seen as a radical reactionary and a sentimental traditionalist; he has been blamed for
making the Negro a scapegoat for the destruction of the legend-
ary Old South; and he has been called a bigot and a "nigger
lover."

No intelligent appraisal of Faulkner's views on the Negro
can be achieved without a consideration of all his nonfiction
statements concerning race relations. Obviously an examination of these statements should also consider the circumstances
surrounding their composition, their relation to the preceding
and subsequent statements, the audiences to whom they were
addressed, and the reactions they elicited. The intention of this
study is to attempt such an appraisal. Although the major focus
will be on the nonfiction of William Faulkner, some attention
first will be paid to his fiction in order to demonstrate the historical accuracy of his characterization of the Negro and to
show the parallels between his fiction and his nonfiction statements on race relations. It is hoped that this procedure will not
only offer an understanding of the mind of the author but will
also elucidate certain problems arising from the criticism of
a major theme in his work.

---

[6] "Ex-Aristocrat's Emotional Education," *The Saturday Review of Literature* 31
(Sept. 25, 1948), 8.

Slavery: The Primal Curse

The contemporary Southern race problem has its roots, of course, in the institution of slavery, and Faulkner has indicated both implicitly, in his fiction, and explicitly, in his public statements, that he considers slavery as a curse on the South. For example, in *Absalom, Absalom!* (p. 21) Rosa Coldfield feels that there is a "fatality and curse on the South" as well as on her own family, as though some ancestor of hers "had elected to establish his descent in a land primed for fatality and already cursed with it." It is the same curse that alters the relationship between Roth Edmonds and his "foster brother," Henry Beauchamp, "The old curse of his fathers, the old haughty ancestral pride based not on any value but on an accident of geography, stemmed not from courage and honor but from wrong and shame" (p. 111). In "The Bear" (*Go Down, Moses*, 257-258) Ike sees the plantation system as accursed ("this plantation and all the life it contained was chattel and revokeless thrall to this commissary store"), and he cries out to Fonsiba's husband "Don't you see? This whole land, the whole South, is cursed, and all of us who derive from it, whom it ever suckled, white and black both, lie under the curse?" (p. 278) Although Walter Sullivan, Peter Swiggart, and Ursula Brumm[1] have seen the curse as incorporating ownership of the land as well as the

---

1 Walter Sullivan, "The Tragic Design of *Absalom, Absalom!*," *South Atlantic Quarterly* 50 (Oct. 1951) 559; Peter Swiggart, *The Art of Faulkner's Novels* (Austin, 1962), pp. 175-177; Ursula Brumm, "Wilderness and Civilization: A Note on William Faulkner," *Partisan Review* 22 (Summer 1955), 347.

institution of slavery, Faulkner himself, when asked about the recurrent theme of "the curse of the South" in his fiction, replied, "The curse is slavery, which is an intolerable condition —no man shall be enslaved—and the South has got to work that curse out" (*Faulkner in the University*, p. 79).

Much of Faulkner's fiction is concerned with the many problems that arose as a result of the impact of slavery upon Southern society. For instance, slavery caused a caste system to be developed within both the white and Negro races which had socio-psychological effects long after emancipation. Slavery also caused peculiar attitudes toward "racial purity" which resulted in nightmarish phobias concerning miscegenation. Although slavery had the tendency to imbrute the conscience of many Southerners, there were those who saw the practice as an example of man's inhumanity. Faulkner has portrayed such individuals in his fiction. The father of Reverend Hightower, for instance, though "born and bred . . . in an age and land where to own slaves was less expensive than not to own them" (*Light in August*, p. 409) not only refused to own slaves but also refused to benefit from any labor done by a slave. The ancestors of the Southern "moderate," Gavin Stevens, owned no slaves, Goodhue Coldfield *(Absalom, Absalom!)* repudiates slavery, and Uncle Buck and Uncle Buddy *(Go Down, Moses)* free those slaves who will accept freedom and play a ritualistic game with those who do not. There were also many examples of genuine devotion between master and slave, and Faulkner has also portrayed such relationships in his fiction, particularly in *The Unvanquished*.

The practice of Negro enslavement was not restricted to white men, for the Indians also kept slaves. Faulkner makes references to the Indian as slaveholder in "Red Leaves," "A Justice," "A Courtship," "The Old People," and *Requiem for a Nun*. Although there is much humor in "Red Leaves" and "A Justice," it is nevertheless apparent that the Indians' treatment of their Negro slaves was inhumane. Faulkner indicates that the presence of the Negro slaves in the Indian community constituted a definite social problem. For instance, in "Red Leaves" (*Collected Stories*, p. 314) Three-Basket complains of the changes caused by the adoption of the white man's practice of Negro enslavement. His complaint is echoed by an old Indian (p. 323):

> "This world is going to the dogs," he said. "It is being ruined by white men. We got along fine for years and years, before the white men foisted their Negroes upon us. In the old days the old men sat in the shade and ate stewed deer's flesh and corn and smoked tobacco and talked of honor and grave affairs; now what do we do? Even the old wear themselves into the grave taking care of them that like sweating."

In aping the ways of the white man, the Indian chief, Doom, has acquired too many slaves: "Doom began to acquire more slaves and to cultivate some of his land, as the white people did. But he never had enough for them to do."[2] Ultimately the mass of idle Negroes become such a strain on the tribe that the Indian hierarchy gather "in squatting conclave over the Negro question" (p. 319). The Indians decide that they cannot eat the slaves, for there are too many of them, and "that much flesh diet is not good for man."[3] Issetibbeha suggests that a few Negroes could be killed and not eaten, but another member of the council argues that "They are too valuable; remember all the bother they have caused us, finding things for them to do." Finally the Indians decide that they must do "as the white men do": raise more Negroes by clearing more land to make corn to feed them, then sell them. So the Indians clear the land with the Negroes, plant it in grain, and begin to engage in Negro slave trade (pp. 319-320). Underlying the humor and irony of "Red Leaves" is Faulkner's implicit statement that the institution of slavery destroyed the proper relationship between the Indian and the land. But slavery also caused the Indian to exhibit the same callousness as did the white man in his treatment of the slaves. There is, for instance, the same disdain based on a concept of racial superiority. In "Red Leaves" (p. 316) Three-Basket and his companion discuss the Negroes'

---

2 "Red Leaves," p. 318. See also "A Justice," p. 345, and "A Courtship," p. 379.
3 The irony here is somewhat reminiscent of Swift's "A Modest Proposal." In an earlier incident in "Red Leaves" an Indian remarks that in his youth he had eaten Negro flesh, but that it was bitter. His companion says that the Negroes "are too valuable to eat, anyway, when the white men will give horses for them" (p. 314).

unwillingness to be buried with their dead masters. The slaves constantly flee when their masters die—they "cling" to life and cause much trouble for their pursuers, but then the Negroes are "a people without honor and without decorum," mere "savages" who "cannot be expected to regard usage" (that is, the Indian practice of burying the slave with his deceased master). In "Red Leaves" the Indians regard the Negroes as animals—"they are like horses and dogs" (p. 314), and Doom entertains his guests by coursing his Negro slaves with dogs (p. 319).

The male slave is often denied his right as a husband and father when an Indian wishes to exercise the *droit de seigneur*. In "A Justice" a slave's wife is impregnated by one of the Indians, but Ikkemotubbe makes light of the situation by telling the husband, "You should be proud of a fine yellow man like this" (p. 357).[4] This story gives a different version of the paternity of Sam Fathers than the one contained in "The Old People" *(Go Down, Moses)*. In "The Old People" it is Ikkemotubbe (Doom) himself who impregnates Sam's mother. Later he pronounced a marriage between the pregnant quadroon and one of the slave men whom he had just inherited, and two years later "sold the man and woman and the child who was his own son to his white neighbor, Carothers McCaslin" (p. 166). Ikkemotubbe's total disregard for his own progeny by a Negro woman is similar to the attitudes exhibited by several white characters in Faulkner's fiction (for example, Carothers McCaslin and Thomas Sutpen).

A peculiar aspect of the institution of slavery in the South was that it developed the idea of class and caste among the slaves and a corresponding resentment among the nonslave-holding poor whites. The division of labor among the slaves (the house and stable as opposed to the field) resulted in subtle gradations of caste and dignity; the Negro groom or butler usually looked down upon the "field nigger," and more impor-

---

4 The plight of the Negro husband in "A Justice" (pp. 354-358) bears comparison with Lucas's dilemma in "The Fire and the Hearth" *(Go Down, Moses*, p. 59). Lucas says: "How to God can a black man ask a white man to please not lay down with his black wife? And even if he could ask it, how to God can the white man promise he won't?"

tantly, the Negro slave, particularly the house servant, looked down upon the nonslaveholding, poor whites or "poor white trash." This sentiment is expressed in the old Negro song: "My name's Sam, I don't give a damn; I'd rather be a nigger than a poor white man."[5]

This slavery-era concept of caste or status, which was to have important effects long after slavery was abolished, is depicted in the fiction of Faulkner. For instance, Faulkner gives many examples of the haughty groom or butler affronting poor whites. In "Wash" the Sutpen slaves regard Wash Jones as "white trash," and Wash never attempts to enter the Sutpen house because he is afraid "some black nigger" would refuse him admittance. Wash resents a "world in which Negroes, whom the Bible told him had been created and cursed by God to be brute and vassal to all men of white skin, were better found and housed and even clothed than he and his"—a world "in which he sensed always about him mocking echoes of black laughter" (*Collected Stories*, p. 538). In *Absalom, Absalom!* Thomas Sutpen's tragic "design" is begun when he is turned away from a mansion by a liveried slave. Sutpen's family and friends lived in cabins "not quite as well built and not as well kept and preserved as the ones the nigger slaves lived in" (*Absalom, Absalom!*, p. 228). There was always an undercurrent of antagonism between the poor white females and the Negro women who passed on the road. For example, Sutpen's sisters looked at the Negro women with a kind of speculative antagonism "not because of any known fact or reason but inherited, by both white and black . . . and which was not quite explainable by the fact that the niggers had better clothes, and which the niggers did not return as antagonism or in any sense of dare or taunt but through the very fact that they were apparently oblivious of it, too oblivious of it" (p. 230).

The cause of the antagonism between the Negroes and the poor whites was primarily economic. The slaves were not in competition with each other but were, in a sense, in league with

5 Quoted in V. L. Wharton's *The Negro in Mississippi, 1865-1890*, Vol. 28 of *The James Sprunt Studies in History and Political Science* (Chapel Hill, 1947), p. 216.

the planters in economic competition with the small farmer. Then, too, slaves often became skilled craftsmen of various kinds, and the practice of hiring these artisans out by the day or job not only supplemented the income of the slaveholders, but also hindered the rise of skilled white labor.[6] The basis for contemporary racial strife is still essentially economic, and Faulkner himself has consistently maintained this view when discussing the reasons for anti-Negro sentiment in the South.[7]

Since the slave was the property of the rich and influential white slaveholders, he was given the full protection of the laws. "The poor white, at times not so well housed or clothed as the slave, still had two great distinctions to cling to and preserve. He was a white man, and free; the Negro was black, and a slave."[8] Emanicipation removed one of these distinctions, and it became obsessively important for the poor white to maintain the other distinction after the Negroes were freed. The demand for "white supremacy" had its true origin with the poor whites, for "the slogan 'white supremacy' really means 'poor white supremacy,' for this term accurately represents the people most concerned in that valorous movement, and the end which they sought to achieve."[9] Many Mississippi politicians, such as John Rankin, James Eastland, James K. Vardaman, and Theodore Bilbo, built their careers by catering to the racist sentiments of this group. In his essay on Mississippi for *Holi-*

---

[6] See Rupert B. Vance, "Racial Competition for the Land," in Edgar T. Thompson, ed., *Race Relations and the Race Problem: A Definition and an Analysis* (Durham, 1939), p. 101.

[7] In ten of his statements recorded in *Faulkner at Nagano* (Tokyo, 1956), Faulkner alludes to the economic basis for racial strife; see pages 5, 48, 77, 98, 99, 129, 166, 167, 168, 169. Faulkner voiced the same opinion in his address to the Southern Historical Association in 1955, in his interview with Russell Warren Howe, and in his essay "On Fear: The South in Labor." Howe himself forcefully argues the economic basis for racial antagonism in "Prejudice, Superstition and Economics," *Phylon* 17 (Oct. 1956), 215-226.

[8] Wharton, p. 216.

[9] C. E. Cason, "Middle Class and Bourbon," in W. T. Couch, ed., *Culture in the South* (Chapel Hill, 1935) p. 497. See also Gunnar Myrdal, *An American Dilemma* (New York, 1944), pp. 597-599. Myrdal points out that at the time of Emancipation, ninety-five per cent of the wage-earning jobs in the secession states were held by freedmen; after Emancipation, political power was added to their economic power and the poor-white reaction was to band together electorally and in terrorist organizations to enforce disenfranchisement and to limit the Negro to the most menial of jobs.

day magazine (April 1954, p. 35) Faulkner described the people who, like the Snopes clan in his fiction,

> elected the Bilboes and voted indefatigably for the Varda-
> mans, naming their sons after both; their origin was in bitter
> hatred and fear and economic rivalry of the Negroes who
> farmed little farms no larger than and adjacent to their own,
> because the Negro, remembering when he had not been free
> at all, was therefore capable of valuing what he had of it
> enough to struggle to retain even that little and had taught
> himself how to do more with less: to raise more cotton with
> less money to spend and food to eat and fewer or inferior
> tools to work with: this, until he, the Snopes, could escape
> from the land into the little grubby side street stores where
> he could live not beside the Negro but on him by marking
> up on the inferior meat and meal and molasses the price
> which he, the Negro, could not even always read.

If the slave looked down on the poor whites, he tended to look up to the rich, slaveholding whites, who possessed what the Negro termed "quality." The respect that the Negroes had for the upper class whites persisted after the emancipation, for they now looked to the white man of "quality" to protect them from the poor whites, who began to rise in power.[10] Faulkner has recorded this attitude in his *Collected Stories*. For example, the scorn for the poor white hosts of his masters exhibited by the Negro groom in "Mountain Victory" is characteristic of the attitude of Negroes after the Civil War, as is the treatment of poor whites by the butlers in "Barn Burning" (p. 11) and "Shall Not Perish" (p. 106). Similarly, the Negro servant Elnora in "There Was a Queen" always considers her white mistress, who has married into the Sartoris family, as "town trash" (p. 729).

This post Civil War attitude of the Negro toward the white person of quality doubtlessly stems from the antebellum mas-ter-slave relationship, a relationship which, incidentally, is not so much a part of the moonlight and magnolia myth as is often supposed. The failure to understand that this relationship

---

[10] See Bertram W. Doyle, *The Etiquette of Race Relations in the South* (Chicago, 1937), pp. 158-160.

often led to ties not only of loyalty but of love has caused many critics to misinterpret certain implications in Faulkner's *The Unvanquished*. Although *The Unvanquished* is primarily concerned with the maturation of young Bayard Sartoris, it also obliquely examines the condition of the slaves during the final years of the Civil War and its immediate aftermath. The book is not one of Faulkner's finest, but it is certainly better than many critics have contended. I will not attempt to defend the literary merits of *The Unvanquished* here, but simply point out what I believe to be critical misconceptions concerning Faulkner's treatment of the Negro slave in this book. The most serious misreading of the novel concludes that Faulkner writes nostalgically of the plantation system, with its faithful ("good") Negroes, and that he portrays (unsympathetically) such "ungrateful" Negroes as Loosh, who go against the system in their desire to be free. This critical attitude is represented by such writers as Louis Kronenberger, who, in his review of the book in *The Nation*,[11] wrote:

> The twisted heritage which the Confederate South bestowed upon its descendants is something few of them have renounced. It has got into their blood, and all that their weakened minds can do is resort to a rather vague, rueful, and inadequate irony. The truer irony is that they are its victims, forever driven on to commemorate their loss of Eden . . . The South languishes in race infantilism. The South is a fetishist because of something that disrupted its childhood; it goes on fondling a faded gray uniform with epaulets, a sword put up in its worn tired scabbard.

Similarly, Earle Birney, in his review of *The Unvanquished*, contends that Faulkner subscribes to the same views held by his slaveholding ancestors and that he is insensitive to the humanity of Negroes.[12] It should be remembered, however, that the narrator of the stories is not Faulkner but Bayard Sartoris, and if Bayard is nostalgic in the early sections of the book it is because he was a young boy at the time the incidents occurred.

---

11 *The Nation*, 146 (Feb. 19, 1938), 212, 214.
12 Earle Birney, "Two William Faulkners," *The Canadian Forum* 18 (June 1938), 84-85.

It is quite natural then, that the earlier incidents in the book are recorded sentimentally, particularly those concerned with the halcyon days of Bayard's youth, when he played with his Negro companion, Ringo. In those days the boys thought nothing of the difference in the color of their skins:

> Ringo and I had been born in the same month and had both fed at the same breast and had slept together and eaten together for so long that Ringo called Granny "Granny" just like I did, until maybe he wasn't a nigger anymore or maybe I wasn't a white boy anymore, the two of us neither, not even people any longer . . . . (pp. 7-8)

> That's how Ringo and I were. We were almost the same age, and Father always said that Ringo was a little smarter than I was, but that didn't count with us, anymore than the difference in the color of our skins counted. (p. 91)

In "Ambuscade," the first story in *The Unvanquished*, the two playmates are totally ignorant of the issues involved in the Civil War—the war was something fought far away, in Virginia or Tennessee—and when Loosh shouts "Gin'ral Sherman gonter sweep the earth and the race gonter all be free," Bayard naively picks up the cry: "It's General Sherman and he's going to make us all free!" (pp. 25-26). Later, Ringo exhibits fear when the Yankees are coming, but Bayard admonishes him by saying, "Do you want to be free?" as if freedom were not only alien but a threat, and Ringo joins his white playmate in shooting at a "Yankee bastud." Loosh, however, is fully aware that he is a slave, and when he talks of freedom he gets a look on his face "which resembled drunkenness but was not."

When the Yankees occupy the area the Union colonel is courtly in the elaborate courtesy he extends to Granny. Melvin Backman feels that this world, where decency still prevails, is one of make-believe—and "the make-believe is not entirely Bayard Sartoris', it is William Faulkner's."[13] Backman oversimplifies when he states that "since the prevailing point of view remains that of the slaveholder, Loosh's departure is felt to be a desertion of the Sartorises in the time of their need. The

---

13 *Faulkner: The Major Years* (Indiana University Press, 1956), p. 115.

story's concern for the Negro is only momentary; its chief concern is for the Sartorises" (p. 115). Similarly, Ralph Ellison writes that "sometimes in Faulkner the Negro is simply a villain, but by an unconsciously ironic transvaluation his villainy consists, as with Loosh in *The Unvanquished*, of desiring his freedom,"[14] and Irving Howe, in his *William Faulkner* (p. 122) contends that Loosh is "singled out for an uneasy kind of ridicule" and that his rebelliousness is not taken seriously. But if the narrator (Bayard) feels that Loosh's actions represent a betrayal, the careful reader may perceive yet another aspect of the situation (p. 85):

"Loosh," Granny said, "are you going too?"

"Yes," Loosh said, "I going. I done been freed; God's own angel proclamated me free and gonter general me to Jordan. I don't belong to John Sartoris now; I belongs to me and God."

"But the silver belongs to John Sartoris," Granny said. "Who are you to give it away?"

"You ax me that?" Loosh said. "Where John Sartoris? Whyn't he come and ax me that? Let God ax John Sartoris who the man name that give me to him. Let the man that buried me in the black dark ax that of the man what dug me free." He wasn't looking at us; I don't think he could even see us. He went on.

Loosh's attitude (and those of the masses of Negroes who press toward the imagined River Jordan) indicates that Faulkner in no way intends to portray all slaves as happy with their lot, yet Backman contends:

For the most part, the Faulkner of *The Unvanquished* idealizes and oversimplifies the Southern past. Various Southern myths are embedded in the stories: for example, that the slave was a contented member of Southern society, that hence the South was a victim of Yankee meddling and aggression, and that the slaveholder of the Old South was generally motivated by the humane and Christian considerations of a Granny Millard and not, of course, by the self-interest of

---

[14] Ralph Ellison, *Shadow and Act* (New York, 1964), pp. 42-43.

an Ab Snopes or Grumby. The stereotypes to which the author clings suggest some fundamental unwillingness to confront reality. (p. 119)

But the final story in *The Unvanquished* ("An Odor of Verbena") indicates that Bayard, now twenty-four, has had a glimpse of reality, which leads him to repudiate a code which often led to violence. The romanticism and naiveté of his childhood had led him to idolize his father—a dashing colonel of Cavalry—but as early as the first section (p. 11) Bayard indicates that he now knows better. He is now more objective in his appraisal of his father (and what he represented); "An Odor of Verbena" is filled with references to his father's "violent and ruthless dictatorialness and will to dominate" (p. 258), to his "intolerant eyes which . . . had acquired that transparent film which the eyes of carnivorous animals have" (p. 266), to his cynicism (p. 266), and to his "intolerant heart" (p. 272). This final section of the book, then, is a rejection of the myth of the plantation South.

But to return to Backman's objections to Faulkner's handling of the Negro in *The Unvanquished*: in his discussion of "Skirmish at Sartoris," (*The Unvanquished*, pp. 215-242) Backman states:

> Never once in the story—or, for that matter, in the entire volume—does the author truly consider whether the Negro too may be entitled to human rights. The "good" Negro, like Ringo, remains loyal to his white masters and even fights for his "nigger" status. As a boy, Ringo is considered almost one of the family; and since the book holds on to the feeling of a boy's world, the picture of the Negro-white relationship is essentially idyllic rather than realistic. (p. 118)

Ralph Ellison has also objected to Faulkner's characterization of Ringo, "who uses his talent not to seek personal freedom but to remain the loyal and resourceful retainer."[15] But the "faithful retainer" is not merely a figment of Bayard's (or Faulkner's) imagination, nor is it part of the "Southern myth." Bell I. Wiley has an excellent discussion of the type in his

---

15 *Shadow and Act*, pp. 42-43.

Southern Negroes, 1861-1865. In the chapter entitled "Body Servants" (pp. 134-145) Wiley points out that the relations between the master and his body servant were usually characterized by mutual affection. The personal servant, says Wiley, was generally chosen from a line of Negroes which had been associated with the family for a long time and who would feel a responsibility for the protection of the master (p. 142). Instances of disloyal or traitorous conduct on the part of the body servant were rare, and there are many testimonies to their firm devotion. Wiley's study also establishes the credibility of the Negro groom in "Mountain Victory" (*Collected Stories*, pp. 745-777), who has taken care of his master during four years of fighting in the Civil War. In explaining such conduct on the part of Negro slaves, Wiley writes:

> There were a number of factors which influenced the slaves' conduct during the war, one of the most pertinent of which was that of personal attachment. Those Negroes who were closely associated with their owners were usually the most loyal under trying circumstances. The body servants of the Confederate soldiers were more intimately associated with their masters than any of the others. In many cases, soldiers and servants had been childhood playmates. Each had a genuine affection for the other, which was cemented by common exposure and hardship in the army. No class of slaves had as good opportunities for desertion and disloyalty as the body servants but none was more faithful. Next in the rank of close association with the whites were the house servants; they were also next in the degree of loyalty. (p 64)

There is also ample evidence to indicate that the loyalty felt by the Negro body servant was reciprocated by the white master. Wiley cites an excellent example (p. 144) taken from the New Orleans *Daily Picayune* of July 4, 1885:

> When the remains of Governor Allen of Louisiana were interred in the State House grounds in 1885, a letter which he had written to his body servant, Vallery, just a year after the close of the war was read as a part of the ceremony. In this missive, significant for the light which it throws on the

affection engendered by the soldier-servant relation, the governor, after expressing satisfaction with good reports of Vallery, said: "I am also glad to hear that you have not forgotten me, for I think of you very often, not only as my faithful servant in former days, but as my companion in arms and on the battle-field. God bless you, Vallery. I don't know that I shall ever see you again, for . . . I am now starting on a long and painful journey to Paris to see if I can't get well. I would like so much to have you go along to assist me and cheer me up in my exile, but I have not the means to pay your expenses. You must be temperate and prudent, and industrious and save your money. If I am ever a rich man again, I will help you and make you comfortable for life . . . . Goodbye Vallery . . . . You were ever true to me, and I will never, never, forget your services.

Although Saucier Weddel, the Confederate officer in Faulkner's "Mountain Victory," refers to his Negro body servant as "my boy," he is very solicitous of his comfort. For example, although Weddel can no longer drink whiskey, he requests some for his servant. He has also cut the sable lining from his coat to wrap around the Negro's feet, and he refuses to escape and leave his inebriated servant behind when it is apparent that his own life is in danger. The delay caused by the servant's drunkenness results in the death of Weddel.

Backman's charge that nowhere in *The Unvanquished* does Faulkner truly consider whether the Negro may be entitled to human rights is unfair. From a strictly literary standpoint, of course, it would have been an artistic failure to have Bayard launch into a discussion of civil rights amidst the recollections of his boyhood. But if Faulkner refuses to grind any personal axes concerning Negro disenfranchisement in the South, he does illustrate that the plight of the Negro slave, both before and immediately after emancipation, was deplorable. Freed from slavery, the Negroes found themselves uprooted and homeless. There is irony as well as humor in Ringo's remark, "I ain't a nigger any more. I done been abolished" (p. 228), but there is great pathos in the scene depicting the Negroes' crazed rush into the river. When Granny warns Philadelphy not to go with Loosh and the other Negroes, saying "Don't you know he's leading you into misery and starvation," Philadelphy begins to cry. "I knows hit," she says. "I knows whut they tole him can't be true. But he my husband. I reckon I got to go with him" (p. 86). The tragedy is that the Negroes believe the promises made to them by their emancipators and begin their hopeless exodus. The magnificent scene in which the Negroes, in their headlong rush to freedom, are beaten back by the scabbards of their liberators (pp. 119-121) reflects (without editorializing) actual conditions shortly after emancipation. The Negroes' former masters are unable to help them, and their presence proves an embarrassment to their liberators. Faulkner's story should be compared with a contemporary account given in *Maj. Gen. William T. Sherman, and His Campaigns:*

> Thousands of negro women join the column, some carrying household trucks; others, and many of them there are, who bear the heavy burden of children in their arms, while older boys and girls plod by their sides. All these women and children are ordered back, heart-rending though it may be to refuse them liberty. (pp. 330-331)

Similarly, Granny Millard's prophetic warning to Philadelphy, "Don't you know he's leading you into misery and starvation," should also be compared to contemporary accounts. For example, Wiley writes that on January 30, 1865, Nathaniel P. Banks, the commander of the Department of the Gulf, wrote William Lloyd Garrison of the miseries of the displaced slaves herded together in the camps:

> Their condition was that of abject misery. I have myself seen at Baton Rouge in one of these Negro quarters, or contraband camps as they were called, one hundred and fifty men, women and children—in every possible condition of misery—cooking, eating, drinking, sleeping, sickening and dying in one room, with a fire built in the center of the floor without chimney, where all phases of this sad history occurred. The same scene was witnessed at every military post. (*Southern Negroes*, p. 211)

Wiley states that the Negroes herded together in these camps died by the thousands, those who were employed on government-leased plantations received treatment little better than that which they received under the old regime, and those who entered military pursuits were dealt with in a manner more becoming to slaves than freedmen.

In *The Tangled Fire of William Faulkner* (pp. 101-102) William Van O'Connor objects to Faulkner's ignoring, in "A Skirmish at Sartoris," the implications of the historical fact of Negro disenfranchisement:

> The marriage is interrupted to enable John Sartoris to drive away carpetbaggers and prevent Negroes from voting. After allowing, in true gallant fashion, two male Burdens . . . to shoot at him first, Sartoris kills them. Sartoris, of course, disenfranchises the Negro—but this is not considered even briefly. The action is turned sharply back to Aunt Louisa's shocked surprise that anything should have postponed her daughter Drusilla's becoming an honorable woman. Perhaps there is a strong case to be made for disenfranchisement at that point in southern history. If there is, Faulkner passed up an opportunity to dramatize it. Sartoris seems a cardboard "hero," moving inside a stereotyped, thoughtless action.

Perhaps the best argument against O'Connor's contention is contained in James B. Meriwether's "Faulkner and the South."[16] Meriwether points out that Faulkner has made considerable effort to show how the carpetbagger officials are easily equated with the burners and looters of wartime. The Burdens' candidate for office, an illiterate ex-slave, is obviously unfit, and the Negroes are "herded" like sheep and held under armed guard in order to secure their votes. But if the Burdens have armed Northern whites intimidating the Negroes, the Southerners have a larger group of armed ex-cavalrymen; if the Burdens take the ballot box inside the hotel, away from the public square, John Sartoris takes the box to his own home for the election; and if the Burdens shoot first, it is obvious that

---

[16] James B. Meriwether, "Faulkner and the South," in *The Dilemma of the Southern Writer*, ed. Richard K. Meeker (Farmville, Virginia, 1961), pp. 143-163.

Sartoris went into the hotel to force them to shoot at him. Thus, though the Burdens were obviously using coercion and bribery to elect an incompetent candidate, Sartoris was also wrong in killing them and in rigging the election at his own home and appointing his fiancée voting commissioner. As Meriwether so ably points out, Faulkner has not ignored the disenfranchisement of the Negro but has "meticulously set the act of disenfranchisement into a context where a mixture of rights and wrongs must be considered" (p. 158). If Faulkner has not concentrated specifically on the plight of the Negroes in the account of the election skirmish, he has at least implicitly indicated that in the struggle for votes between Northern Republicans and Southern Democrats, the good of the Negro was totally overlooked by both sides. And here again Faulkner is being historically accurate. John Hope Franklin, in his *From Slavery to Freedom*[17] writes:

> The struggle between the organized Southern whites on the one hand, and the Union League, Freedmen's Bureau, federal troops, and Negroes on the other, was essentially a struggle for political control of the South. From the Northern point of view it was a question of whether the gains of the war were to be nullified by the rebels who had brought the nation to the brink of disaster in 1861. From the Southern point of view it was a question of home rule—a right which they would defend to the end—and of who should rule at home, which they felt was largely academic since Negroes were not qualified. As surely as the struggle between 1861 and 1865 was civil war, so was the conflict from 1865 to 1877, with all the more bitterness and hatred, but less bloodshed. The peace was being lost because of the vigorous efforts of both parties and sections to recruit their strength from the ruins of war. Peace could not prevail in such warlike circumstances.

In "Skirmish at Sartoris" Ringo seems to sense the implications of the struggle. He tells Bayard about the two Burdens from Missouri, who have a patent from Washington to organize

[17] John Hope Franklin, *From Slavery to Freedom—A History of American Negroes* (New York, 1966), p. 324.

"the niggers into Republicans," and how Colonel Sartoris and the other Southern whites were trying to prevent it. "Naw, Suh," he says. "This war ain't over. Hit just started good. Used to be when you seed a Yankee you knowed him because he never had nothing but a gun or a mule halter or a handful of hen feathers. Now you don't even know him and stid of the gun he got a clutch of this stuff [dollar scrip] in one hand and a clutch of nigger voting tickets in the yuther" (p. 229).

It may be seen, then, that there is a historical basis for Faulkner's presentation of the master-slave relationship (which is certainly not *always* seen as pleasant). Faulkner was in no way intending to sentimentalize the slavery system nor, as has been contended, was he attempting to perpetuate the myth of the plantation South.

Miscegenation

If critics have misinterpreted Faulkner's handling of slavery, many have also erred in their evaluation of Faulkner's attitude toward miscegenation. The persistent theme of miscegenation in Faulkner's fiction has led many critics to conclude (erroneously) that Faulkner labors under a regional (and racial) phobia—a fear of the "horrifying conjunction" of the white female and the Negro. Thus, Charles I. Glicksberg, in "William Faulkner and the Negro Problem,"[18] writes that "No Faulkner novel is complete without its compounded plot of horror, seduction, illegitimate children, rape, incest, perversion, but overriding all these elements is the theme of Negro blood as a source of defilement, an abomination. It is an obsession present not only in the horror-haunted mind of Faulkner but also in the collective psyche of the South." And Maxwell Geismar, in *Writers in Crisis* (pp. 179-180) writes:

> So we see, just as Faulkner was punishing the northern woman in "Light in August," now he threatens the entire western hemisphere with the rape of the Negro. And what better images, after all, could the artist have found to ex-

---

[18] *Phylon* 10 (1949), 157.

press his discontent—this great hatred of the entire complex of modern northern industrial society—than the Negro and the Female? The emancipated negro who to the southern writer is the cause of the destruction of all he held dear. And now showing this negro as Joe Christmas, as Jim Bond, as the inhuman criminal,[19] the degenerate who will dominate the civilization which freed him, Faulkner proclaims at once his anger and his revenge upon those who have destroyed his home. What more appropriate symbol than the woman, who to the southern writer is the particular treasured image of the bygone, cavalier society he is lamenting and lost in: the southern Lady, elevated and sacrosanct, the central figure of the southern age of chivalry, of those gallant agrarian knights who, very much like Quixote, went forth in 1861 to perish in combat with the dynamo.

According to Geismar, Faulkner's use of miscegenation is "the last step in his sequence of discontent": Faulkner mates the Female with the Negro, the savage for whom the Southern Lady was sacrificed, and "spawns out of his modern union the colored degenerate who is to reign supreme, the moronic emperor of the future" (p. 180). Melvin Seiden, in "Faulkner's Ambiguous Negro,"[20] examines what he calls "Faulkner's lurid racist theme" in *Absalom, Absalom!* Faulkner's sympathetic treatment of Clytie, says Seiden, is "exactly what the liberal who suspects him of racism would expect" (p. 685), while Charles Bon is "a figure who seems to remain in Faulkner what he has always been in popular fiction and cinema: the enemy within, the alien who must be destroyed lest he destroy us all, the scourge who must be made a victim" (p. 676). Seiden contends that "the point, of course, is that the racist's double standard smiles at the *droit de seigneur,* while the black man's 'lusting' after white women is an abomination that can only lead to Shreve's sardonic prophecy of the Jim Bonds inheriting the earth" (p. 686). Even Irving Howe, in his often perceptive *William Faulkner, A Critical Study* writes:

---

[19] I will indicate later that Faulkner is actually sympathetic with his Negro criminals.

[20] *Massachusetts Review* 4 (Summer 1963), 675-690.

Mulattoes are living agents of the "threat" of miscegenation, a "threat" which seems most to disturb Faulkner whenever he is most sypathetic to the Negro. All rationalizations for prejudice having crumbled, there remains only an inherited fear of blood-mixture. The more Faulkner abandons the "ideas" of the folk mind in relation to Negroes, the more does he find himself struggling with the deeper phobias of the folk mind. In two of the novels where miscegenation is a major theme, *Light in August* and *Absalom, Absalom!*, it arouses a painfully twisted response. (p. 128)

The above critical statements represent serious misinterpretations of Faulkner's intent in his presentation of racial interbreeding. Actually, there is some support for the argument that Faulkner looks upon an ultimate (but far distant) amalgamation of the races as the final solution for the race problem.[21] Both *Absalom, Absalom!* and "Delta Autumn" contain strong hints that racial conflict would be ended by racial mixing, and in 1955, speaking to a group at the Tokyo American Cultural Center, Faulkner said "in a few hundred years the Negro in my country will vanish away. He will be assimilated into the white race simply because there are more white people" (*Faulkner at Nagano*, p. 166). Also, in the interview with Russell Howe in 1956, Faulkner said "In the long view, the Negro race will vanish in 300 years by intermarriage. It has happened to every racial minority everywhere, and it will happen here."[22] In 1958, however, Faulkner made a somewhat contradictory statement. Asked at a conference at the University of Virginia if he did not see the best solution to the integration problem to be race assimilation. Faulkner replied, "No, sir, I don't think that would solve many problems. The same amount of bickering would go on and they would find another subject for it. I think that the only thing that will solve that problem is not integration but equality" (*Faulkner in the University*, p. 227). In any event, miscegenation was an in-

---

[21] See, for instance, Agnes Louise Moreland's unpublished dissertation "A Study of Faulkner's Presentation of Some Problems That Relate to Negroes" (Columbia University, 1960), pp. 102-111.

[22] *The Reporter* 14 (Mar. 22, 1956), 19.

evitable result of slavery, and it is quite natural that it is a major issue in Faulkner's treatment of slavery in the South. When Faulkner treats of unions between whites and Negroes during the period of slavery, he is indicating the chattel status of the slave woman and the inhumanity of the white man; when he treats of the issue of such unions (particularly in the post-emancipation period) he often uses mulattoes symbolically. Above all, it should be remembered that in Faulkner's handling of miscegenation, the Negro is inevitably portrayed as the victim and not the offender.

In *Absalom, Absalom!* and *Go Down, Moses,* Faulkner examines miscegenation as the by-product of the slavery system, under which a young man could ride up and beckon the watching overseer and say "Send me Juno or Missylena or Chlory" and then ride on into the trees and dismount and wait (*Absalom,* p. 110) or an old man could "summon, because she was his property, a human being because she was old enough and female, . . . get a child on her and then dismiss her because she was of an inferior race" ("The Bear," *Go Down, Moses,* p. 294). John Hope Franklin, in his *From Slavery to Freedom* (p. 203), indicates the extent to which Negro women were subjected to the whims and desires of white men:

> Some relationships were the result of physical compulsion on the part of the white man, and if resistance was offered it was frequently beaten back in the most vicious manner. Many slave women carried scars to their graves which had been inflicted by their owners or other whites when resistance was offered to their advances. Other slave women did not resist, either because of futility, the prestige that such a relationship would bring, or because of the material advantages that might accrue from it. Children born of such unions were slaves; and the result of such extensive mixing was that by 1850 there were 246,000 mulatto slaves out of a total slave population of 3,200,000. By 1860 there were 411,000 mulatto slaves out of a total slave population of 3,900,000.

The practice of white men maintaining young Negro women in a state of concubinage was so prevalent in New Orleans that it almost gained social acceptability. The keeping of an octoroon mistress gave status to the young blades of New Orleans. In *Absalom, Absalom!* Charles Bon describes the practice, with much romantic rationalization in its defense, to his provincial half-brother (pp. 114-118). But despite Bon's sophistical arguments about saving the "one sparrow," who "but for us would have been sold to any brute who had the price, not sold to him for the night like a white prostitute, but body and soul for life to him who could have used her with more impunity than he would dare to use an animal, heifer or mare" (p. 116), it is still obvious that the octoroon mistresses were merely hybrid chattel, "creatures taken at childhood, culled and chosen and raised more carefully than any white girl, any nun, than any blood mare even" (p. 117) to love and be beautiful and divert their white keepers. The position of the children resulting from these relations was not necessarily any better than the mulattoes produced by the planters in the rural areas: "the child, the boy, sleeping in silk and lace to be sure yet complete chattel of him who, begetting him, owned him body and soul to sell (if he chose) like a calf or puppy or sheep" (p. 114).

Contrary to what some critics have contended, Faulkner's concern with miscegenation is not due to any fear that it will lead to race pollution. Primarily, he is sympathetic with its victims, that is, the offspring of black-white unions who, because of prevailing attitudes toward racial interbreeding, are made to suffer. Indeed, it is not miscegenation but the miscegenation complex that is the real concern of Faulkner. In *Absalom, Absalom!*, for instance, Thomas Sutpen's subscription to the Southern code of racial purity is so binding that he repudiates his first wife and child (Eulalia and Charles Bon). Sutpen's "grand design," which is based to a great extent on the role he intends to assume in Southern society, precludes a male heir with even "a drop" of Negro blood. The code does allow him to acknowledge the paternity of his daughter Clytie, the result of his union with a slave, and to maintain her as a servant within his household, without endangering his status as a Southern *seigneur*. A similiarity might be seen in the elder Bayard Sartoris' treatment of Elnora (see *Sartoris* and "There Was a Queen").

In *Absalom, Absalom!*, miscegenation, or rather the attitudes toward it, severs father from son, brother from brother, and lover from loved one. If Thomas Sutpen can justify his repudiation of his wife Eulalia and his son Charles on the basis of their mixed blood, Charles himself can disavow any obligations incurred as a result of the morganatic "ceremony" between himself and the octoroon mother of his son. When Charles' brother Henry argues "But there is still the marriage," Charles replies (p. 118): "Have you forgot that this woman, this child, are niggers? You, Henry Sutpen of Sutpen's Hundred in Mississippi? You, talking of marriage, a wedding, here?"

The rejection of the offspring resulting from white-Negro interbreeding is also illustrated in "The Bear." In this work, Isaac McCaslin slowly discovers the miscegenation of his grandfather, Carothers McCaslin, who had a daughter (Tomasina) by his slave woman, Eunice. Later he adds incest to miscegenation by impregnating Tomasina, who dies in giving birth to a boy (Terrel or "Tomey's Turl"). In his will, Carothers McCaslin leaves money to Turl, "flinging almost contemptuously, as he might a cast-off hat or pair of shoes, the thousand dollars which could have had no more reality to him under those conditions than it would have to the negro, the slave" whom he had sired by his own daughter (p. 269). And even the thousand dollars was "cheaper than saying my son to a nigger." Similarly, in *Absalom, Absalom!*, Sutpen eases his own conscience by leaving his repudiated wife and son in considerable wealth, but refuses to say "my son" to Charles Bon. In constantly juxtaposing slavery-era white men with their rejected Negro kinsmen, Faulkner indicates how the miscegenation complex constitutes another barrier to the brotherhood of man. He also indicates how even the mere threat of miscegenation can cause much tragedy and bloodshed. In *Absalom, Absalom!*, Henry kills his half-brother Charles Bon—whom he loved more than his father and sister—because of the miscegenation that would occur if Charles were to marry their sister Judith; "it's the miscegenation, not the incest" which Henry cannot bear (p. 356). "You are my brother," exclaims Henry, but Charles reminds him, "No I'm not. I'm the nigger that's going to sleep with your sister. Unless you stop me, Henry" (pp. 357-358). In "Mountain Victory," the otherwise gentle young mountaineer becomes desperate not because his sister may give herself to the handsome Confederate officer but because he might be a Negro: "The boy cried quietly, with a kind of patient and utter despair. 'I told her if you was a nigra, and if she done that—I told her that I—.' "[23] And in *Light in August* the mere suspicion that he might have Negro blood causes Joe Christmas's tragedy (it is never known for certain whether or not his father is part Negro).

The Legacy of Slavery— Racism in the Modern South

Most of Faulkner's fictional and nonfictional treatment of the race question is focused upon the role the Negro plays in the modern South. Faulkner is aware that contemporary white attitudes toward the Negro, as well as the conduct of the Negro himself, have their origins in slavery and that the South's guilt for slavery was no more exonerated by its loss of the Civil War than the problem of race relations was ended by the Emancipation Proclamation. In *The Unvanquished* (p. 228), Ringo tells Bayard, "I ain't a nigger any more. I done been abolished." But as Wendell Phillips pointed out, the Emancipation Proclamation freed the slaves but ignored the Negroes. The North was, of course, in no better position than the South to make citizens of the former slaves. Indeed, Lincoln himself was reluctant to free the slaves, and earnestly hoped that the freed slaves would return to Africa. In a speech made in 1858 Lincoln said:

> I will say then that I am not, nor ever have been in favor of bringing about in any way the social and political equality of the white and black races—that I am not nor ever have been in favor of making voters or jurors of Negroes, nor of qualifying them to hold office, nor to intermarry with white people; and I will say in addition to this that there is a physi-

---

[23] *Collected Stories*, p. 767.

cal difference between the white and black races which I believe will forbid the two races living together on terms of social and political equality. And inasmuch as they cannot so live, while they do remain together, there must be the position of superior and inferior and I as much as any other man am in favor of having the superior position assigned to the white race. (*the Political Writings of Abraham Lincoln,* ed. A. B. Lapsley, IV [New York, 1966], 1.)

Even such a militant abolitionist as William Lloyd Garrison viewed slavery as a moral and not a social problem. Because he was interested in the immorality of slavery and not the condition of the slaves, he considered the race question solved once the Emancipation Proclamation was signed. Garrison's sentiments should be compared to that of Nathaniel Burden in *Light in August.* Burden tells his daughter Joanna that she should continually strive to elevate the "black shadow" (the Negroes) but that she could never succeed in lifting it to her level, for "the curse of the black race is God's curse" and thus cannot be removed by human effort. Thus Burden, a northern liberal who had worked earnestly in the behalf of emancipated slaves, indicates his belief in the inferiority of the Negroes.

Although there were notable exceptions, the vast majority of Negroes were indeed emotionally and economically unprepared for a new role in American society. What resulted was that the legal bondage of the former slaves was replaced by a debt peonage, and a more subtle form of slavery, sharecropping, was instituted. Yet the Negroes were "kept in their place" by pressures other than economic; as Tocqueville noted, "there is a natural prejudice that prompts men to despise whoever has been their inferior long after he has become their equal." As early as 1837 Tocqueville realized that the only means by which ancient cultures maintained slavery was fetters and death, "while the Americans of the South of the Union have discovered more intellectual securities for the duration of their power. They have employed their despotism and their violence against the human mind." The Southerners, he continues, have adapted measures to deprive the Negro "even of his desire for freedom."

Keeping Negroes uneducated and impoverished also kept them servile and dependent, and a unique system of role playing was established upon this fact. Humility, servility, and dependence were seen as qualities of the "good" Negro, and white Southerners were willing to put up with laziness and inefficiency where these characteristics were present. By 1888, George Washington Cable could write that the South "tolerates, with unsurpassed supineness and unconsciousness, a more indolent, inefficient, slovenly, unclear, untrustworthy, ill-mannered, noisy, disrespectful, disputatious, and yet servile domestic and public menial service than is tolerated by any other enlightened people," and a more recent observer, John Dollard, writes that one of the factors supporting the rigid caste structure of Southern society is "the relatively indulgent behavior permitted to Negroes in lieu of the struggle to achieve higher social status."[24]

Any sign of ambition or attitude of independence is considered symptomatic of the "biggity ideas" of the "bad" Negro. On the other hand, promiscuity, indolence, lying, petty thievery, and other "sorry" characteristics are overlooked if they are accompanied by obsequiousness, for all are considered to be part of the nature of the "good" Negro (that is, one who knows his "place"). Two of Faulkner's most memorable Negro males, Sam Fathers and Lucas Beauchamp, refuse to play the role assigned to them by white society. In his relations with white men, Sam Fathers bore himself with "gravity and dignity and without servility or recourse to that impenetrable wall of ready and easy mirth which negroes sustain between themselves and white men" ("The Old People," *Go Down, Moses*, p. 170). In *Intruder in the Dust*, Lucas Beauchamp is a constant source of frustration to the white community, who are determined to "make him be a nigger." Even the Negro community in this novel resents Lucas's arrogance; the young Negro Aleck Sander expresses the sentiment of the other Negroes when he says "It's the ones like Lucas makes trouble for everybody" (p. 85). Yet even the fiercely independent Lucas

24 John Dollard, *Caste and Class in a Southern Town* (Garden City, New Jersey, 1949).

can, on occasion, resort to masking his real feelings behind the impenetrable wall of the Negro: "Without changing the inflection of his voice and apparently without effort or even design Lucas became not Negro but nigger, not secret so much as impenetrable, not servile and not effacing, but enveloping himself in an aura of timeless and stupid impassivity almost like a smell" (*Go Down, Moses*, pp. 59-60).

The peccadilloes of the "good" Negro are looked upon with smiling condescension by the paternalistic white Southerner, who believes that he understands the Negro as no outsider can. But despite the white Southerner's claim that he "knows" the Negro, the contrary seems to be true, for so well has the Negro learned to play the ritualistic game of race relations that he can actually use his apparent obsequiousness and sycophancy as weapons against the white man. For example, playing the cap-pulling darkie or the clownish fool can cause the white man to accept inferior work. In 1929, Robert R. Moton, the head of Tuskegee Institute, said:

> Much of what is regarded as racially characteristic of the Negro is nothing more than his artful and adroit accommodation of his manners and methods to what he knows to be the weakness and foibles of his white neighbors. Knowing what is expected of him, and knowing too what he himself wants, the Negro craftily uses his knowledge to anticipate opposition and to eliminate friction in securing his desires.[25]

This "artful and adroit accommodation of his manners" by the Negro is discussed at length in Bertram W. Boyle's *The Etiquette of Race Relations in the South* (Chicago, 1937). In many cases such action results in the "mask" of the smiling menial, as described by the poet Paul Laurence Dunbar in his "We Wear the Mask":

We wear the mask that grins and lies,
It hides our cheeks and shades our eyes,—
This debt we pay to human guile;
With torn and bleeding hearts we smile,

---

[25] Quoted in Charles E. Silberman, *Crisis in Black and White* (New York, 1964), p. 97.

And mouth with myriad subtleties.
Why should the world be overwise,
In counting all our tears and sighs?
Nay, let them only see us, while
  We wear the mask.

We smile, but, O great Christ, our cries
To thee from tortured souls arise.
We sing, but oh the clay is vile
Beneath our feet, and long the mile;
But let the world dream otherwise,
  We wear the mask!

The mask can, of course, hide more than pain. Boyle (p. 158) writes that "the Negro makes use of supererogatory flourishes and embellishments of behavior. He has learned that such persons (whites who insist on respect because of their race) will pay, in one way or another, for deference. In such circumstances he will emphasize the ritual and the external forms, although sentiment may occasionally be lacking. They speak publicly . . . of how they love the white people, but privately, the majority of them sing another tune."[26] Another aspect of the mask is described in Bernard Wolfe's "Uncle Remus and the Malevolent Rabbit."[27] Wolfe describes the function of Brer Rabbit and other folk symbols in siphoning off hatred before they completely possess consciousness. The tales, like so much of folk culture, act as a kind of "psychic drainage system" which makes it possible for Uncle Tom not only to retain his façade of grinning Tomism but also, to some degree, to believe in it himself.

But if the "false face" aspect of Negro conduct has allowed many white Southerners to see only the Negro they wished to see, it has also prevented sympathetic whites from understanding the real Negro beneath the mask. Negroes are so convinced

---

[26] Walker Vessels, the Black revolutionist in LeRoi Jones' play, "The Slave," shuffles onto the stage at the beginning of the drama in the guise of a field hand. He sheds this guise during the action of the play, in which a white couple is killed, and reverts to it at the final curtain.

[27] *Commentary* 8 (July 1949), 31-44.

of the necessity of the mask that they seldom remove it.[28] Two Negro writers, Ralph Ellison and Richard Wright, have made reference to this in their works. In Ellison's *Invisible Man*, for instance, a Negro college president chides a young student for his conduct with a white trustee of the college. "You're black and living in the South—did you forget how to lie? . . . Why, the dumbest black bastard in the cotton patch knows that the only way to please a white man is to tell him a lie!" And Richard Wright, in *Twelve Million Negro Voices*, describes the Negroes' creation of "new types of behavior and new patterns of psychological reaction" in their relations with the whites:

We strove each day to maintain that kind of external behavior that would best allay the fear and hate of the Lords of the Land, and over a period of years this dual conduct became second nature to us and we found in it a degree of immunity from daily oppression. Even when a white man asked us an innocent question, some unconscious part of us would listen closely, not only to the obvious words but also to the intonations of voice that indicated what kind of answer he wanted; and automatically, we would determine whether an affirmative or negative reply was expected, and we would answer, not in terms of objective truth, but in terms of what the white man wanted to hear.

If a white man stopped a black on a southern road and asked: "Say there, boy: It's one o'clock, is it, boy?" the black man would answer: "Yessuh."

---

[28] This characteristic of Negro conduct has seriously hampered historical, sociological, and psychological studies of Negroes. For example, the psychologist Kent S. Miller has stated that psychological understanding of the Negro is still in its formative stages, primarily because of the Negro's suspicion of the whites: "The Negro himself has been . . . [a] major stumbling block in the path of better understanding of his temperament and personality organization. In any experiment it is difficult to obtain data without the cooperation of the subject. There is reason to believe that the Negro frequently brings an unconscious attitude of resistance into experimental settings just as many are believed to bring this attitude into all of their contacts with whites. This tendency to 'cover up' has been observed in psychiatric treatment and in other settings a number of times. Since this is primarily an unconscious resistance, it is difficult to deal with and probably will present problems for the investigator for some time to come." See "Psychological Characteristics of the Negro," *The Negro in American Society* (Tallahassee, Florida, 1958), p. 25.

And if the white man asked, "Say, it's not one o'clock, is it boy?" the black man would answer, "Nawsuh."

And if the white man asked: "It's ten miles to Memphis, isn't it, boy?" the black man would answer: "Yessuh."

And if the white man asked: "It isn't ten miles to Memphis, is it boy?" the black man would answer: "Nawsuh."

Always we said what we thought the whites wanted us to say.[29]

Much of the Negro's behavior, or action, is in reality a *reaction* to the actions of other individuals in his society. Despite the fact that the American Negro represents a distinct ethnic group, the Negro himself often has difficulty in defining just what he is. Stripped of his past and totally severed from any culture except that of the United States, the Negro is a "creation" of American society; as W. E. B. DuBois phrased it, "there is nothing so indigenous, so completely 'made in America' as we [the Negroes]."[30] Yet America has refused to accept its own creation, and the Negro has been faced with problems of identification that no white man has had to undergo. It is quite natural that the Negro's self-esteem suffers because of the unpleasant image of himself which he constantly receives from the actions of others.[31] But perhaps more psychologically damaging than the ubiquitous, overt prejudice is the pernicious social ostracism that denies the very existence of the Negro. So pervasive is this subtle denial that the Negro begins to doubt his own personality—perhaps beneath the mask, he thinks, there is no face at all. This condition of "facelessness," as James Baldwin describes it, has become an obsessive concern of Negro writers. W. E. B. DuBois expressed it as a sense of never being heard, Ralph Ellison uses the metaphor of invisibility,[32] and James Baldwin expresses it in the phrase "nobody knows my name."[33] In Richard Wright's "Man of All Work," a Negro male who cannot find a job

---

[29] Ralph Ellison, *Invisible Man* (New York, 1952), p. 107; Richard Wright, *Twelve Million Negro Voices* (New York, 1941), p. 41.

[30] *Dusk of Dawn* (New York, 1940), pp. 310-331.

[31] See Abram Kardiner and Lionel Ovesey, *The Mark of Oppression* (Cleveland, 1962).

[32] See his *Invisible Man.*

[33] *Nobody Knows My Name* (New York, 1961).

dresses himself in his wife's clothes and gets a job as a cook. He justifies his action to his horrified wife by saying: "Who looks that close at us colored people anyhow?" (*Eight Men*, [New York, 1962], p. 124.)

The Negro is convinced that the whites control everything in such a manner as to keep him in his place, and his self-esteem suffers from a deep-rooted sense of powerlessness and impotence. Coupled with this there is often a feeling of self-hatred, which manifests itself in the use of hair straighteners, skin bleaches, and a concern with the caste of color.

Faulkner illustrates this sense of futility on the part of the Negro in many of his fictional characters. For example, Nancy, in "That Evening Sun," rationalizes her promiscuity by repeating "I ain't nothing but a nigger. It ain't none of my fault." Nancy is, of course, illustrating her acceptance of the white man's callous evaluation of the Negro. More importantly, "That Evening Sun" illustrates how totally certain white people misunderstand the Negro. The attitude of the jailer towards Nancy's attempted suicide ("no nigger would try to commit suicide unless he was full of cocaine, because a nigger full of cocaine wasn't a nigger any longer") should be compared with similar attitudes expressed in other Faulkner short stories. The deputy in "Pantaloon in Black" cannot accept the presence of strong human emotion in a grief-stricken young Negro ("when it comes to the normal human feelings and sentiments of human beings, they might just as well be a damn herd of wild buffaloes") nor can Uncle Buck, in "The Bear," believe that a Negro is capable of suffering enough to commit suicide ("Who in hell ever heard of a niger drownding him self"). In short, "Pantaloon in Black," "The Bear," "Was," "The Fire and the Hearth," and "That Evening Sun" all illustrate the white man's inability to believe in the Negro's capacity to love, hate, or suffer. Even Chick Mallison, in *Intruder in the Dust*, does not immediately perceive that *"You dont have to not be a nigger in order to grieve."*

The inability of the whites to see through the mask of the Negro results in an inevitable estrangement of the races. The seriousness of this estrangement is discussed by Faulkner in his "A Word to Virginians" (*Faulkner in the University*, p.

211). It is possible, he says, that the white race and the Negro race can never really like or trust each other because the white man can never really know the Negro. This is "because the white man has forced the Negro to be always a Negro rather than another human being in their dealings, and therefore the Negro cannot afford, does not dare, to be open with the white man and let the white man know what he, the Negro, thinks."

Some attention should also be paid to Faulkner's handling of the Southern law-enforcement officers' attitude toward the Negro criminal. Like many other of his fictional characters, Faulkner's judges and policemen illustrate a bias which denies the humanity of the Negro; for example, the deputy in "Pantaloon in Black" says that Negroes "aint human." The Negroes are often used as scapegoats for the collective guilt of the white community, or they are framed to cover a white criminal's guilt. In *The Hamlet*, for instance, Lump Snopes plans to cover the murder committed by his kinsman Mink Snopes by playing on the race prejudice of the white community.

> I threw the suspicion right onto the nigger fore Hampton could open his mouth. I figger about tonight or maybe tomorrow night I'll take a few of the boys and go to the nigger's house with a couple of trace chains or maybe a little fire under his feet. And even if he don't confess nothing, folks will hear that he has done been visited at night and there's too many votes out here for Hampton to do nothing else but take him on in and send him to the penitentiary, even if he cant risk hanging him, and Hampton knows it. So that's all right. (p. 267)

Similarly, in *Intruder in the Dust*, Lucas is framed for a murder committed by a white man. Lucas, a smoking gun in his hand, is found standing near the body of a murdered white man. Because of the prejudice against his race, no one takes the trouble to ascertain whether or not Lucas's gun was of the same caliber that killed the white man, and he is immediately accused of the murder and almost lynched. And in *Light in August*, Lucas Burch tries to free himself from suspicion of murdering Joanna Burden by frantically appealing to the same racial prejudice that governs the irrational actions of both lynch mobs and the lawmen when he shouts at the marshal "accuse the white man and let the nigger go free. Accuse the white and let the nigger run" (p. 85). The Negroes are aware that guilt is often determined by the complexion of one's skin; in *Sartoris*, an old Negro is afraid to extricate the white Bayard Sartoris from an overturned car because "white folks be sayin' we done it" (p. 207).

Intruder in the Dust:
Faulkner as Polemicist

Before turning to Faulkner's nonfiction statements concerning race, some attention should be paid to *Intruder in the Dust* (1948), for this novel is doubtlessly Faulkner's most important "fictional" treatment of the Negro problem. Written at a time when racial tensions were mounting, stronger civil rights legislation was impending and the clamor for states' rights was beginning, *Intruder in the Dust* is both novel and tract. Indeed, the novel suffers considerably from the polemics of the lawyer, Gavin Stevens, whose pronouncements concerning the race issue constitute a traditional stand for states' rights. Some critics have seen Gavin Stevens as representing the attitude of Faulkner, and there is some basis for this contention. Stevens' statements about states' rights and Sambo are at once liberal and reactionary, and they bear a strong resemblance to the pattern of contradictions exemplified in Faulkner's statements in the interview with Russell Warren Howe in which almost every sentence contradicts the one preceding it. Although Faulkner has often been described as what was once known as a "moderate," he refers to himself as a "liberal" in the same interview in which he assumes the stance of a states' righter. These contradictions, however, are not as puzzling as they at first appear; actually they are somewhat typical of the sentiments expressed by many Southern liberals in the late forties and early fifties. The parallel between Faulkner and these men is implicit in a statement he made in 1948 during a conversation with John K. Hutchen, a columnist for the New York *Herald Tribune Weekly Book*

Review: "I'm a states' rights man. Hodding Carter's a good man, and he's right when he says the solution of the Negro problem belongs to the South." In this sentiment Gavin Stevens would also concur.

In 1948 there were many Southerners who, along with Faulkner, "hated the intolerance and injustice: the lynching of Negroes not for crimes they committed but because their skins were black . . . the inequality: the poor schools they had then when they had any, the hovels they had to live in unless they wanted to live outdoors: who could worship the white man's God but not in the white man's church; pay taxes in the white man's courthouse but couldn't vote in it or for it . . . ,"[34] but who nonetheless realized that what the Civil War and nearly a century of racial conflict had failed to correct could not be resolved instantly (and without violence) by new legislation. "It is a situation," says Faulkner, "that simply cannot be changed overnight for the reason that it is not basically a moral problem. It is an economic problem, and if it were changed overnight it would mean turmoil, confusion, because it would be an upset of a working economy" (*Faulkner at Nagano*, p. 99).

Gavin Stevens speaks of the homogeneity of the Southern people, of the necessity of defending Lucas-Sambo from the Outlanders (*i.e.*, the North and East and West) who would fling him decades back "not merely into injustice but into grief and agony, and violence, too, by forcing on us laws based on the idea that man's injustice to man can be abolished overnight by police" (pp. 203-204). Such sentiments coincide with the many public statements Faulkner was to make in the 1950s. Even such words as "homogeneity," "outlander," and " to confederate," which are so recurrent in the conversation of Gavin Stevens with his nephew, are repeated in the many non-fiction statements made by Faulkner on the civil rights issue.

Again, Gavin Stevens insists that the precipitate and impatient actions of the outlanders could (at bayonet point) force many Southerners "who do begrieve Lucas' shameful condition and would improve it" and eventually abolish it, to ally

---

[34] "Mississippi," *Holiday* 15 (April 1954), 44.

themselves with those objectionable elements with whom they have "no kinship whatever" in defense of a principle which they "begrieve and abhor." This possibility is repeated even more explicitly by Faulkner in the Howe interview. Faulkner told Howe that he did not like enforced integration any more than he liked enforced segregation, and that if he had to choose between the United States government and Mississippi, he would choose the latter. "What I'm trying to do now," he said, "is not to have to make that decision." As long as there is a middle of the road, he continued, he would stay on it, "but if it came to fighting I'd fight for Mississippi against the United States even if it meant going out into the street and shooting Negroes."[35]

The implications of this statement, and Faulkner's later retraction of it, will be discussed in full elsewhere in this text. It should be noted here, however, that Faulkner's loyalty to his region often obtrudes into his otherwise liberal and humanitarian statements; again, in the Howe interview, he said, "I will go on saying that the Southerners are wrong and that their position is untenable, but if I have to make the same choice Robert E. Lee made then I'll make it."[36] Faulkner states that his grandfather had made the same decision when he fought in the Civil War, not in "defense of an ethical position but to protect his native land from being invaded." In order to understand fully *Intruder in the Dust* one must also understand the extent to which Faulkner is caught up in the collective mind of the South. This collective psyche, which exerts such an impact on contemporary Southern writers, has its origins in the aftermath of the Civil War. In describing its impact on the writing of James Branch Cabell, Edmund Wilson writes:

> We Northerners do not, I believe—unless we have been a good deal in the South—really grasp the state of mind of the Southerners. We have always made a point, in our relations with them, of disregarding what we call the Civil War, they of remembering it and calling it the War Between the States. We like to assume that the United States is an integrated,

[35] *The Reporter*, Mar. 22, 1956, p. 19.
[36] *Ibid.*

homogeneous, and smoothly functioning nation, and unless we are professional historians, we succeed in forgetting completely that the former Confederacy was an occupied country to a greater or lesser extent for twelve years after the War, and that it has still a good deal of the mentality of a resentful and rebellious province under some such great power unit as the old Austro-Hungarian Empire. Except when an issue arises so troublesome that it cannot be ignored —such as that of the recent Supreme Court ruling against racial segregation in the schools—we hardly realize how deep and how virulent, from a long-standing sense of grievance, runs the instinct toward repudiation of any responsibility on the part of the South to that federal government of states which are by no means so completely united as the Northerner likes to suppose. The Northerner does not take account of the extent to which the Southerner—if not overtly, at least among other Southerners and in his own most intimate being—disassociates himself from the North. For a writer, this has special consequences.[37]

The consequences of this disassociation with the outlander is certainly reflected in Faulkner's writings, and is quite apparent in his address "To the Youth of Japan," in which he makes repeated references to "my country, the South." In drawing parallels between the South and postwar Japan, Faulkner said, "Our land, our homes were invaded by a conqueror who remained after we were defeated; we were not only devastated by the battles we lost, the conqueror spent the last ten years after our defeat and surrender despoiling us of what little war had left. The victors in our war made no effort to rehabilitate and reestablish us in any community of men or of nations" (*Nagano*, p. 185). It is this same deep-felt loyalty to homeland and suspicion of outside force which motivates many of the statements of Gavin Stevens in *Intruder in the Dust* (and of Faulkner in the Howe interview).

But *Intruder in the Dust* does not offer only Stevens' (and Faulkner's) opinion on intervention from outside the South,

---

37 "The James Branch Cabell Case Reopened," *The New Yorker*, Apr. 21, 1956, p. 141.

but also indicates what can be done from within. The rationalizations and theorizings of the lawyer are juxtaposed with the actions of his young nephew, Chick Mallison. In a discussion of *Intruder in the Dust* at one of the Nagano seminars, Faulkner said that to theorize about an evil was not enough, that someone must do something about it—"even if it took a little boy and an old frightened woman" (*Nagano*, p. 97). Indeed, the main action of the book, a young boy's attempt to prevent the lynching of an innocent Negro (an effort which also necessitates the overcoming of his inherited prejudice) illustrates a point made by Faulkner in his conferences at Nagano, Japan, that "if the problem of black and white existed only among children, there'd be no problem" (*Nagano*, p. 76).

Intruder in the Dust represents Faulkner's strongest statement in his fiction regarding the racial crisis in the South. As racial tensions continued to increase in the decade following the publication of this novel, Faulkner was moved to write a great many nonfiction pronouncements on race relations. These views, expressed in conferences, speeches, and public letters, offer valuable insight into what Faulkner felt about the Negro. It is ironic, however, that these statements caused Faulkner to be vilified by both the Northern and Southern press, and to be the recipient of threatening telephone calls and hostile letters (see *My Brother Bill*, p. 268). Obviously Faulkner's opinions must be viewed in their historical context, for unless some understanding of the circumstances surrounding the composition of these statements is realized, no adequate appraisal is possible.

The Turner-Whitt Murder Trial

The earliest instance of Faulkner's public condemnation of bigotry is a 1950 letter to the editor of the Memphis *Commercial Appeal*, in which he deplored what he felt to be a miscarriage of justice in Mississippi. In March of that year three white men, Leon Turner, 38, Windol Whitt, 25, and his brother, Malcolm Whitt, 27, were tried for the slaying of three Negro children (the penalty for murder in

Mississippi at that time was either the electric chair or life imprisonment, the penalty to be set by the jury).

On the night of December 22, 1949, Turner and the Whitt brothers had kicked in the door of a Negro dwelling, terrorizing the family as they searched for money. Then they went to the Harris cabin and continued their reign of terror, but the inhabitants of the first house notified the authorities and Turner and the Whitt brothers were apprehended while still in the Harris cabin. The brothers were charged with the illegal possession of whiskey and housebreaking, as was Turner, who was also charged with attempted rape. The trio were confined in the Attala County Jail but escaped on the night of December 30 and fled into the woods. Nothing further was heard from them until the night of January 8, when Turner is reported to have said to the Whitt brothers, "Let's go clean 'em [the Harris family] out."[38]

The three children were killed January 9, 1950, in a shanty occupied by a Negro tenant farmer, Thomas Harris, and his family. Harris charged that Turner and the Whitt brothers arrived at his cabin early on the morning of January 9 and said that they were "going to have Verline Thurman" (Harris's fourteen-year-old stepdaughter) or they would "kill the whole damn family." Then, while the Whitt brothers guarded the front and back doors, Turner shot Harris in the back, then shot four of the children. Harris was paralyzed from the chest down; three of the children, four-year-old Ruby Nell Harris, eight-year-old Mary C. Burnside, and twelve-year-old Frankie C. Thurman, were killed; and Verline Thurman was shot in the breast and arm. Harris's wife escaped with her nine-month-old baby in her arms.

News of the murder quickly spread, a posse was formed, and Leon Turner and Windol Whitt were captured with the aid of bloodhounds (Malcolm Whitt had surrendered himself earlier). Turner, who had earlier been sentenced to ten years in the state penitentiary for assault and battery, had just finished serving his sentence a few months before the January murder of the children. There was much speculation in the

[38] Memphis *Commercial Appeal*, Mar. 12, 1950, sec. 2, p. 12.

newspapers about the trial, for it might have resulted in the first execution of a white man (or men) for the killing of a Negro in Mississippi.

On March 21 Turner was sentenced to life, although ten jurors had argued for the electric chair. Five days earlier Windol Whitt had also been given a life sentence. Malcolm Whitt pleaded guilty to manslaughter in the death of the four-year-old and was sentenced to ten years in the state penitentiary. Thomas Harris, who had testified from a stretcher during the trials, died on April 12.

Faulkner was deeply disappointed in the verdict of the jury, and was moved to write a letter to the Memphis *Commercial Appeal* (March 26, 1950). Faulkner begins by saying that Mississippians should feel concern and grief about the verdict, which showed the world (the "outland people") that their state equated the murdering of three children with the robbing of three banks or the stealing of three automobiles. Faulkner is afraid that those people like himself who, because of their love for Mississippi, its customs, and its people, had defended the state from attack by the outlanders, might have been wrong. Faulkner particularly deplores the action of the two members of the jury who "saved the murderer," and hopes that whatever reason they had for doing so will be sufficient to free them from nightmares about "the ten or fifteen or so years from now when the murderer will be paroled or pardoned or freed again, and will of course murder another child, who it is to be hoped— and with grief and despair one says it—will this time at least be of his own color."

It was inevitable that Faulkner's letter would evoke responses from fellow Mississippians, some of whom were already incensed at Faulkner's criticism of Southern injustice in his fiction.[39] An example of this attitude is a letter written by Clayton Stephens and published in the *Commercial Appeal* on April 2, 1950. Stephens expresses his resentment of Faulkner's's stand on the Turner murder trial, and asks "If Turner's victims had been white children, would Faulkner have been so

---

[39] For a listing of the responses to Faulkner's *Commercial Appeal* letters, see the bibliography.

excited about the jury verdict?" Evidently, states Stephens, Faulkner would have preferred the children to have been white, and he wonders if Faulkner would have written a letter about the trial had Turner been a Negro. Stephens implies that Faulkner would give a Negro special consideration just because he is a Negro, and argues "Wait until a Negro attacks some white woman and see if Mr. Faulkner will write a letter condemning the Negro." Stephens contends that the Negro situation in the South "may be good material for a best-selling novel, but as for advancing true brotherhood, it is false. The sullen, disrespectful Negro in *Intruder in the Dust* didn't help solve the race issue."

Faulkner answered Stephens in a letter published in the April 9, 1950, *Commercial Appeal*. In this letter Faulkner says that he protests any drunken man murdering three children, regardless of the race of the man or the children. The people who injected race issues into this tragedy, says Faulkner, were the same people who created a situation which furnished Northern critics the opportunity to protest with "a hundred times the savagery and a thousand times the unfairness and ten thousand times less the understanding of our problems and grief for our mistakes." Faulkner concludes his letter with the statement that Southerners should have some satisfaction that a native of the region (and a sharer in its errors) should have the opportunity to criticize it first. It should be noted that in the first letter Faulkner twice refers to the "outlander," and in the second to the Northern critics. In *Intruder in the Dust*, Gavin Stevens often uses the expression *outlander* in his argument that the South should absolve itself of racial prejudice—without interference or pressures from the outside.

Faulkner's next public statement on the race issue is a press release on March 27, 1951, concerning the Willie McGee trial. The intention of this statement is to refute certain misquotations appearing in the press after Faulkner was interviewed by a delegation of women from the Civil Rights Congress. On November 2, 1945, a man broke into the home of Mrs. Troy Hawkins, the wife of a Laurel, Mississippi, postal worker, and raped her. Mrs. Hawkins had been up most of the night with her small daughter, who was ill. About 4:00 A.M. she dozed off with her daughter in bed (her husband was asleep in an adjoining room). She was later awakened by a man who approached her bed and threatened to cut her throat if she gave alarm. The man then raped her and fled. The only information that Mrs. Hawkins was able to furnish the police was that the rapist was a Negro and that he had been drinking, but a neighbor testified that at approximately 4:30 A.M. she had seen a Negro male drive away in a grocery truck that had been parked near the Hawkins house. A grocery firm also reported that a truck, the truck's Negro driver, Willie McGee, and twenty dollars of the firm's money were missing. A search was begun for McGee,

who was arrested the next afternoon. McGee, married and the father of four children, immediately confessed orally and, later, in writing. Two Negroes who were with McGee at the time of his arrest reported that they had been drinking with him until 3:00 A.M. on the morning of the alleged assault.

The first trial of the thirty-one-year-old McGee lasted less than a day; the jury found him guilty in $2\frac{1}{2}$ minutes. McGee was sentenced to death in the electric chair, but the Mississippi Supreme Court reversed the conviction on grounds that McGee could not possibly have received a fair trial (the atmosphere at his trial was so emotionally charged that state guardsmen had patrolled the courthouse with fixed bayonets). McGee's second trial was held in Hattiesburg (some thirty miles away from Laurel) and, quite predictably, McGee was again convicted and given the death sentence. The sentence was again reversed, however, this time on the grounds that Negroes were exempted from the grand jury lists.

The Willie McGee case had gained much notoriety by the time of the third trial, and various Communist organizations cabled protests to President Harry S. Truman (see *Nation* 171 Aug. 5, 1950, p. 118), and *Time* reported that the trial had become "sure-fire propaganda, good for whipping up racial tension at home and giving U.S. justice a black eye abroad" (*Time* 47, May 4, 1951, p. 26). According to *Life* magazine, McGee was suddenly "a pawn in a world propaganda war, a symbol with which Communism sought to convince Chinese and Indians and Indonesians that capitalism hates and tortures anyone who is not white" (*Life* 30, May 21, 1951, p. 44).

Time charged that McGee's defense in the third trial was under the control of Bella Abzug and John Coe (who had been brought from New York and Florida) and that these individuals were responsible for a "new and ugly accusation that McGee had been intimate with Mrs. Hawkins for several years and had been framed because he had tried to break off the relationship." According to *Time*, there was no evidence that such a relationship had existed, and that a physician had testified that Mrs. Hawkins had been raped. The overwhelming evidence against McGee was ignored by the defense (see *Time, ibid.; Life, ibid.;* and *Nation* 172, May 5, 1951, p. 421), as was the fact that McGee never took the stand in his own defense. The propaganda value of the trial was prolonged. "Save Willie McGee" rallies were held in cities from Los Angeles to Paris, and pickets, including McGee's wife, marched in front of the White House. McGee mysteriously became a "veteran" (he was never in the Armed Services) and a "union man" (the union he was supposed to belong to was not organized at the time claimed).

When McGee was sentenced to death for the third time the Mississippi Supreme Court called the charges against Mrs. Hawkins a "revolting insinuation and plainly not supported" and denied a third appeal. Willie McGee was scheduled to die on July 27, 1950. The Civil Rights Congress, responding to a series of articles by McGee's wife in the New York *Daily Compass*, sent a delegation to Jackson, Mississippi, to protest to Governor Fielding Wright. Stating that he would not tolerate a mob of "wild-eyed howling Communists," Wright nonetheless agreed to meet with a small delegation of the demonstrators. The day before McGee's scheduled execution, Wright held an executive clemency hearing in the capitol's legislative chambers. Led by Aubrey Grosman, the delegation from the Civil Rights Congress argued that the South's system of racial segregation automatically raised a doubt about whether or not a Negro could receive a fair trial in a rape case. The delegation also noted that McGee had been condemned to die for a crime for which no white man had ever been executed in Mississippi.

On July 27, 1950, only twelve hours before he was scheduled to die, McGee was granted a dramatic reprieve by U.S. Supreme Court Justice Harold H. Burton, who called for a stay of execution until the full court met in the fall and could rule on a petition for review of the case. McGee was transferred from the jail in Laurel, where he had been awaiting execution, to a "mob-proof" prison in Jackson. This action was the result of numerous reports of violence—Grosman was assaulted by a group of men in his hotel room, a reporter from the *Daily Compass* was beaten by a gang and run out of town by police, and members of the Civil Rights Congress had been attacked by mobs in Mississippi. As Communism became more and more identified with the case, the NAACP and other organizations and individuals, despite their sentiments about the trial, withdrew their support. There was a deluge of editorials maintaining that anyone trying to save McGee was helping the Communist cause; the fact that many non-Communists believed in McGee's innocence or that he should not be executed for rape because of his skin color was quite overlooked. Willie McGee was executed at Laurel, Mississippi, in May 1951. The U.S. Supreme Court refused, three times, to review the conviction.

In a brief but carefully worded statement to the press (Memphis *Commercial Appeal*, Mar. 27, 1951) Faulkner disassociated himself from the representatives of the Civil Rights Congress, saying that he had nothing in common with them other than the desire to see Willie McGee live. In his statement Faulkner indicates that the execution of McGee will make him a martyr and notes the tremendous propaganda value of such an execution. The women who came to Mississippi to protest, says Faulkner, are being "used" by the Communists, whose cause "would be best helped with the execution of Willie."

The "Rat Hole" Puzzle

Faulkner's public letters do not always deal with the violence which often attends examples of racial discrimination; sometimes the manifestation of prejudice or bigotry offered Faulkner the opportunity to comment in a light vein. A case in point is the "rat hole puzzle" which Faulkner conceived as a rebuttal to the protests of T. T. Wolstenholme, an irate citizen of Hohenwald, Tennessee. In a letter to the editor of the Memphis *Commercial Appeal* (Feb. 6, 1955) Wolstenholme objects to the attention paid by that newspaper to the predicament of Memphis Negroes. Wolstenholme begins his letter by stating his belief that the white race and "their high morality, as created by the 'Lord,' shall not be eradicated from the face of this earth," and that "all white people should band together as protection or preventative of the lower races taking over and trodding us under." "In your issue of January 31," he writes, "you picture the terrible plight of some of the Negroes in the city of Memphis while it looks to me as though they are too lazy to clean up or nail up a few rat holes. Is it your idea that the white people should go there, clean up and prepare better living quarters for these people?" He goes on to say that in Lewis County, Tennessee, there were some white people who really did need help. Why not send a reporter up here, he asks, "and I will take him around where he can really get pictures of some pathetic cases of helpless and jobless white people." Faulkner answered with a most humorous letter published in the *Commercial Appeal* on February 20, 1955. In this letter, Faulkner wonders if Wolstenholme's suggestion that the white investigating groups should go to Lewis County, where they would find "plenty of white people deserving of their offices," means that "for every rathole Shelby County Negroes have, Lewis County white folks have two?" This cannot be correct, says Faulkner, because "white folks, not being Negroes, are not shiftless; and therefore, for every rathole which a Shelby or Lewis County, Tenn., or a Lafayette County, Miss., Negro has, a Shelby or Lewis County, Tenn., or Lafayette County, Miss., white man can't have any." But this is not true either, because there are more rats than people, and there is always some "inevitable and inescapable point at which the white man, no matter how unshiftless, is going to have one rathole." The problem Faulkner then poses is "at what point on the scale of the Negro's nonratholes does the white man gain or earn one or anyway have one rathole? Is unshiftless twice as unshiftless as shiftless, giving the white man twice as many ratholes as the Negro man, or does this get us into the old insoluble problem in amateur physics about how much is twice as cold as zero?"

The School Desegregation Issue

The following month, however, Faulkner was again writing with obvious concern about the developments in the racial strife in America. That the Supreme Court ruling on the integration of the public schools would evoke further turmoil in the South was inevitable. In 1955, Faulkner obviously felt that the "separate but equal" school system in the South was ineffective as well as unconstitutional, and he tried to appeal to the reason of his fellow Mississippians on this basis. In a letter published in the March 20, 1955, *Commercial Appeal,* Faulkner alludes to the Supreme Court ruling on the integration of public schools and points out that Mississippi's schools were "not even good enough for white people." He also indicates the economic absurdity of maintaining two identical ("separate but equal") school systems, neither of which was adequate. Faulkner contends that Mississippians must realize that the existing schools are not good enough, for the young people of Mississippi themselves prove that when they must go out of the state to receive adequate training in the humanities and in the professions. If the "present state reservoir of education is not of high enough quality to assuage the thirst of even our white young men and women," asks Faulkner, "how can it possibly assuage the thirst and need of the Negro, who obviously is thirstier, needs it worse, else the Federal Government would not have had to pass a law compelling Mississippi (among others of course) to make the best of our education available to him."

Nevertheless, says Faulkner, instead of improving the inadequate white system, Mississippians have raked and scraped to raise additional taxes in order to establish a second system which is, at best, only equal to the first, the result being that the state has "two identical systems neither of which are good enough for anybody."

Faulkner's letter was answered in the March 27, 1955, *Commercial Appeal* by letters from Dave Womack, State Representative from Humphreys County; C. J. Martin of Greenwood, Mississippi; and W. C. Neill of North Carrollton, Mississippi. Womack and Martin contend that Faulkner offers no, practical economic solution to the problem, and all three writers argue that "in proportion to its economic ability, Mississippi is doing the utmost for the education of its youth." In closing his letter, Womack writes "we would like to know how many degrees he [Faulkner] holds from these inferior Mississippi schools, of which he writes."

On April 3, 1955, the *Commercial Appeal* published a letter in which Faulkner answers Womack and Martin by offering an economic solution: to take a portion of the funds necessary to maintain a second system equal to the first, and use it in the creation of a superior school system. This improved school system would then itself "take care of the candidates, white and Negro both, who had no business in them in the first place." The remainder of the funds would be used to establish trade and craft schools for the students eliminated from the academic schools. These students, says Faulkner, would be eliminated from the academic system before they had time "to do much harm in the terms of their own wasted days and the overcrowded classrooms and harried underpaid teachers which result in a general leavening and lowering of educational standards; not to mention making the best use of the men and women we produce."

Faulkner admits that his plan only solves integration and not the impasse of the emotional conflict over it. The letter closes with an answer to Womack's query about Faulkner's educational background. Faulkner states that he is an "old veteran sixth-grader" who holds no degrees or diplomas from any school. Perhaps, says Faulkner, that is why he has too much respect for education to sit quietly and watch it "held subordinate in importance to the color of the pupil's skin."

Faulkner's letter was answered by Representative Womack in the April 10 issue of the *Commercial Appeal*. This letter marks the beginning of the increasingly personal attacks which Faulkner was to receive as a result of his stand on the race question. Womack argues that Faulkner "should have been trying to do something about its [Mississippi's] problems for the past 25 years instead of holding it up to ridicule by the world." Faulkner is further attacked for criticizing the "inferior Mississippi schools." "Inferior indeed!!!," writes Womack, "What other state can boast a sixth grade graduate as a Nobel Prize winner?"

In the same issue of April 10, another Faulkner letter was published. Faulkner had been attacked in print and had also received personal letters criticizing his earlier remarks on Mississippi's educational system. In this letter, Faulkner states that his intention had not been to injure the existing school system, but to take advantage of whatever changes the future might bring. His aim was to raise the schools from "their present condition of being a sort of community of state-supported baby sitters, where the pupil is compelled by law or custom to spend so many hours of the day, with nobody but often under-paid teachers to be concerned about how much he learns." Faulkner suggests that a student's schooling should be fitted to his ability and interest, and that if there must be two school systems, the second should be for pupils ineligible for the first not because of their color but because they are unable or unwilling to do creditable work in the first. Faulkner's views in this letter should be compared with similar remarks he made concerning education while at the University of Virginia (see *Faulkner in the University*, pp. 216-217).

An anonymous letter, signed "STUDENT," also appeared in the April 10 *Commercial Appeal*. The writer praised Faulkner for speaking the truth about the educational system in Mississippi, and continued by stating "I plan to enter Ole Miss next year and I favor Negroes entering that school and other public schools of Mississippi. So long as the races are pulling against each other (educationally that is) they will succeed only in pushing both races down." The student closed his letter with the hope that the people of his state "will wake up to the fact if they lower the educational standards of the Negroes as they seem to be now doing they will lower the standards for the whites as well."

In subsequent issues of the *Commercial Appeal*, the student was accused of desiring to "mongrelize the race" and of being ashamed to print his name. Faulkner, however, in a letter in the April 17 *Commercial Appeal*, commends the student for his stand and sympathizes with his fear to reveal his identity. "And what a commentary that is on us," he writes, "that in Mississippi communal adult opinion can reach such emotional pitch that our young sons and daughters dare not, from probably a very justified physical fear, sign their names to an opinion adverse to it." Faulkner feels that many young Mississippians are tolerant, and he calls for a student survey to be conducted to determine their reaction to school integration.

The idea that young people are free from prejudice was again expressed by Faulkner four months later in Japan, where he had gone in August 1955 on the invitation of the Exchange of Persons Branch of the United States Department of State. At the Nagano Seminar, Faulkner said, "If the problem of black and white existed only among children, there'd be no problem. . . . That is, if man for a moment could be set in abeyance and a generation of black children and white children allowed to grow up together, the problem would vanish, I think" (*Faulkner at Nagano*, p. 77).

During a visit to the Tokyo American Cultural Center, Faulkner said that the Negro will have to exercise a great deal of patience for a few more years.

He'll simply have to wait until a few old people in the South die, that's really what will have to happen. When the problem becomes one of the younger people, the problem vanishes, the younger people that have served as soldiers with Negro children, there's no problem, there's no problem among the children, they play together and sleep together and eat together. It's only when they get old and inherit that Southern economy which depends on a system of peonage do they accept a distinction between the black man and the white man . . . . (*Faulkner at Nagano*, p. 167)

At the same meeting in Tokyo, Faulkner contended that the white man's "latent refusal to mix" racially never develops until adulthood:

If you remember that our latent refusal to mix never appeared in youth, in childhood, only in middle age, that in youth and childhood there's no problem, they seem to mix; I grew up with Negro children, my foster mother was a Negro woman, I slept in her bed and the Negro children and I slept in the same bed together. To me they were no different than anyone else. I noticed that with my own children. It's only when the child becomes a middle-aged man and becomes a part of the economy that that latent quality appears. (*Faulkner at Nagano*, pp. 168-169)

Before two years had passed Faulkner was to alter his sentiments on integration and cause a new attack to be leveled against him—this time from the Northern press. A review of some of the events accompanying the Civil Rights movement during these two years, however, will afford an explanation for Faulkner's apparent shift in his position on integration.

On May 24, 1955, about the same time that Faulkner was attacking Mississippi's segregated school system, the Little Rock District School Board approved a plan of gradual desegregation of the races in the public schools of Little Rock, Arkansas. The plan provided for desegregation at the senior high level (grades 10 through 12) as the first stage. Desegregation at the junior high and elementary level was to follow. Desegregation at the high school level was to commence in the fall of 1957, and it was expected that the complete desegregation of the school system would be accomplished by 1963.

While the School Board was proceeding with its plan for desegregating the Little Rock school system, other state authorities began a program to insure the perpetuation of racial segregation in the schools. For example, in November 1956, an amendment to the State Constitution was passed which commanded the Arkansas General Assembly to oppose "in every Constitutional manner the Unconstitutional desegregation decisions . . . of the United States Supreme Court," and in February 1957, a law was passed relieving school children from compulsory attendance at racially mixed schools. The Little Rock School Board and the Superintendent of Schools, however, continued their preparations to carry out the first stage of the desegregation program, and nine Negro children were scheduled for admission in September 1957 to Central High School, a school which at that time had more than two thousand students.

On September 2, 1957, the day before the nine Negroes were to enter Central High, Governor Faubus dispatched units of the Arkansas National Guard to the Central High School grounds and placed the school "off limits" to Negro students. Up to this time, no acts of violence or threats of violence in connection with the carrying out of the desegregation plan had occurred; the Mayor, the Chief of Police, and the school authorities had made no request to the Governor for state assistance. The action of Faubus caused the School Board to request the Negro students not to attend the high school "until the legal dilemma was solved," but on September 3 the District Court ordered the School Board and the Superintendent to proceed with the planned integration.

On the morning of September 4, 1957, the nine Negro children attempted to enter Central High but were prevented from doing so by units of the Arkansas National Guard. The guardsmen, acting under orders from the Governor, stood shoulder to shoulder at the school grounds and forcibly prevented the entrance of the Negro children. They continued this action every school day for the next three weeks. The District Court found that the School Board's plan had been obstructed by the Governor through the use of National Guard troops, and on September 20, 1957, granted a preliminary injunction enjoining the Governor and the officers of the National Guard from preventing the attendance of Negro children at Central High School. The National Guard was then withdrawn from the school grounds. On Monday, September 23, the Negro children entered the school under the protection of the Little Rock Police Department and members of the Arkansas State Police. The children were removed from the school that morning by the officers, however, because the police were having difficulty controlling a large crowd that was demonstrating at the school.

On September 25, President Dwight D. Eisenhower dispatched federal troops to Central High School and the admission of the Negro students was immediately effected. Regular army troops were replaced by federalized National Guardsmen who remained until the end of the school year. Federal troops were still located on the school grounds when, on October 7, 1957, William Faulkner wrote a letter to the editor of the New York *Times* concerning the Little Rock crisis. The letter was published in the *Times* on Sunday, October 13. In a surprising opening paragraph Faulkner said that the tragedy of Little Rock was that it brought out a fact which people could no longer ignore: "that white people and Negroes do not like and trust each other, and perhaps never can."[40] He continues by saying that the important thing now is not that the two races like and trust one another, but that they "federate" together, "show a common front" in order that they may survive as a people and a nation. Faulkner warns that Americans stand alone as the last people unified nationally for liberty in an inimical world which outnumbers them. Americans will endure only if they are willing to federate into a community of "individual free men," and not into a "monolithic mass of a state dedicated to the premise that the state alone shall prevail."

Eight of the Negro children remained in attendance at Central High throughout the school year under the protection of regular army troops or units of the National Guard. The army troops had been replaced by federalized Guardsmen for a little more than three months when, in March 1958, Faulkner was interviewed in New Jersey by Howard Thompson. Faulkner was at Princeton University conducting a two-week session of seminars sponsored by the English Department. During the interview, which was published in the March 8, 1958, New York *Times* (p. 19), Thompson asked Faulkner to comment on the problems arising out of school integration in Little Rock. Faulkner is quoted as saying "It's always been my belief that the white folks and the colored folks simply don't

[40] On Feb. 20, 1958, during a conference at the University of Virginia, Faulkner said "It is possible that the white race and the Negro race can never really like and trust the other; this for the reason that the white man can never really know the Negro, because the white man has forced the Negro to be always a Negro rather than another human being in their dealings, and therefore the Negro cannot afford, does not dare, to be open with the white man and let the white man know what he, the Negro, thinks."

like one another. It seems to me that simple. In making the integration decision, the Supreme Court ignored this." This statement echoes the similar sentiment expressed five months earlier in Faulkner's letter in the New York *Times* of October 13, 1957.

Faulkner told the interviewer that the solution to racial tension is the responsibility of the whites, and then indicated the solution: "The white man must change the Negro from acting and thinking like a Negro. How? The answer is just one word—education." Earlier, in his "If I Were A Negro" (*Ebony*, Sept. 1956, pp. 70-73), Faulkner had advised the Negro leaders to send daily a Negro child to "the white school to which he was entitled by his ability and capacity to go." When the child was refused admittance, he should be forgotten as an individual, but another child should be sent the following day, "to be refused in his turn, until at last the white man himself must recognize that there will be no peace for him until he has solved the dilemma." In the interview with Thompson, Faulkner proposes a similar procedure for white parents: "The integration solution would be for white parents to send their kids back and back again to school with the other race. Until it becomes a habit. Otherwise our two cultures will never meet, except in trivial, every-day matters involving such things as a car or a washing machine."

A close reading of the statements made by Faulkner in 1957-58 will indicate that he has not actually altered his opinion on the necessity of school integration, but that he senses a danger in the Supreme Court's forcing the implementation of its ruling. Several factors had caused the change of emphasis in Faulkner's statements concerning the race issue since 1955.

The Emmett Till Murder

In the spring of 1955, Faulkner saw integration as a moral issue that had too long remained unresolved. His public letters of this period indicate that he still believed that an appeal to right reason, or logic, might move the majority of Southerners, particularly the younger ones, to accept gradually the civil rights of Negroes. By August 1955, however, Faulkner had become alarmed at the attention being drawn to America's racial strife, and he began to see political as well as moral implications in the struggle that was already being labeled a revolution. During his visit to Japan in early August, Faulkner was frequently questioned about the Negro problem, and when in the same month the murder of a young Negro in Mississippi resulted in world-wide criticism Faulkner issued a statement which not once mentions the immorality of the murder but instead contains a warning about the survival of America as a nation.

The murder victim was Emmett Louis Till, a fourteen-year-old Chicago Negro who was visiting his great-uncle near the hamlet of Money, Mississippi. According to testimony given at the murder trial, the boy had directed a "wolf whistle" at Mrs. Roy Bryant, a white woman. At approximately 2:00 A.M. on the morning of August 28, 1955, Till was ordered from his bed and taken from his uncle's cabin by three white men. The boy's body was found three days later in the Tallahatchie River. Till had been beaten and then shot with an Army .45 pistol. A cotton gin fan was fastened to his neck to cause his body to submerge.

The boy's uncle, Moses Wright, identified J. W. Milam and his half-brother, Roy Bryant, as two of the three white men who had abducted the boy from the cabin. Bryant and Milam were acquitted by an all-white jury in Sumner, Mississippi, on September 23, 1955. The jurors said that their verdict was based on a defense contention that the body taken from the river on August 31 was too badly decomposed for positive identification. The defense also suggested that the whole thing was a plot by outsiders to destroy the Southern way of life and to "widen the gap which has appeared between our white and colored people in the United States." Although the outsiders responsible for the plot were not mentioned by name, the local rumor was that it was the NAACP. Till's mother, a government office worker in Chicago, said she was concerned that the murder trial would be used by Communists as anti-American propaganda, as the McGee trial had been.

Bryant and Milam admitted abducting the child, but denied that they killed him. A twenty-man grand jury later declined, however, to indict the two men for the admitted kidnapping. Later, in an interview with William Bradford Huie, Milam admitted killing the boy *(Look,* Jan. 22, 1957, pp. 63-68). Milam said that he had not intended to kill Till when they took him from his uncle's farmhouse—"just whip him and chase him back up yonder," but Till refused to be intimidated and showed the two men pictures of several white girls from his wallet. "What else could I do?" Milam asked. "No use lettin' him get no bigger!" (p. 64).

It is significant to note that neither Milam nor his younger half-brother felt that they had anything to hide. The two men were convinced before the trial that the white community (including the jurors and the defense attorneys) thought they had killed the boy, but since most of the responsible whites in Mississippi had swarmed to their defense, they assumed that the murder had been approved. Faulkner, too, must have assumed what the verdict would be; in a press dispatch on the Till case, released in Rome and carried by American newspapers as a United Press dispatch (see New York *Herald Tribune,* Sept. 9, 1955), Faulkner condemns those responsible for Till's murder, not after the verdict (as in the Turner murder trial), but even prior to the announcement of the date for which the trial had been set.

The main point of Faulkner's statement, however, is *survival* (he uses the word "survive" ten times in eight short paragraphs). Faulkner points out the white race represents only one fourth of the earth's total population of white, brown, yellow, and black races, and that the whites dare not commit acts which the other three-fourths of the human race can challenge—not because the acts are criminal, but because the challengers are not white in pigment. There are also the other Aryan people who are already the enemy of the West because of political ideologies. How can the West hope to survive, asks Faulkner, with "not only all peoples who are not white, but all peoples with political idealogies different from ours arrayed against us—after we taught them (as we are doing) that when we talk of freedom and liberty, we not only mean neither, we don't even mean security and justice and even the preservation of life for people whose pigmentation is not the same as ours?"

The same note of warning was sounded by Faulkner two months later when, on November 10, he was one of three speakers who addressed the twenty-first annual meeting of the Southern Historical Association in Memphis, Tennessee.[41] Again Faulkner makes his plea for racial tolerance not on the basis of morality but on survival. If free men want to continue to be free, says Faulkner, they must "confederate, and confederate fast, with all others who still have a choice to be free—confederate not as a black people nor white people nor pink nor blue nor green people," but as people who still are free.

In this speech, Faulkner explicitly alludes to Communism as a clear and present danger. America, he says, still has an excellent chance to teach the rest of the world that freedom is possible without sending "costly freedom expeditions into alien and inimical places already convinced that there is no such thing as freedom and liberty and equality and peace for all people, or we would practice it at home." America still has this chance because its nonwhite minority, despite a history of inequality, is still on its side.

The Howe Interview

Faulkner's next statements on the race question proved to be the most controversial he ever made. It is unfortunate that the statements which have drawn the most attention—statements which Faulkner later repudiated— are those contained in the 1956 interview with Russell Warren Howe. Jame Baldwin, for example, in his *Partisan Review*

---

[41] The topic of the three speakers was "The Segregation Decisions." Faulkner's address was printed the following morning in the Memphis *Commercial Appeal* (Nov. 11, 1955), p. 8. The speech was again printed, with slight differences in spelling and punctuation, in *The Christian Century* (Nov. 30, 1955), pp. 1,395-1,396, and again printed in a considerably altered and expanded version in a pamphlet entitled *Three Views of the Segregation Decision* (Atlanta, 1956), pp. 9-12.

essay "Faulkner and Desegregation,"[42] twice alludes to the interview, particularly to the business of "shooting Negroes." It is unfortunate that so much attention was focused on this somewhat notorious interview, and so little attention paid to Faulkner's many public letters on integration. Because of the emphasis which has been placed on this interview, however, certain facts should be noted.

On February 21, 1956, Russell Warren Howe, a correspondent for the London *Sunday Times*, interviewed Faulkner concerning the racial problems in the South. The interview was published in the London *Sunday Times* on March 4, 1956,[43] and a variant text appeared in *The Reporter* on March 22.[44] The version of the interview published in *The Reporter* was quoted in *Time* and in various newspapers throughout the country. Reaction on the part of the readers was immediate. One reader felt that the interview made clear that "even the most intelligent and most 'liberal' Southerner is unable to embrace emotionally a national or a Christian viewpoint on this subject, no matter how clearly he sees it intellectually."[45] Most objections were to Faulkner's statement about shooting Negroes—something, as one reader expressed it, "that the most illiterate race baiter would be hesitant about admitting to any reporter." In the interview with Howe, Faulkner had said:

> I don't like enforced integration any more than I like enforced segregation. If I have to choose between the United States government and Mississippi, then I'll choose Mississippi. What I'm trying to do now is not have to make that decision. As long as there's a middle road,[46] all right, I'll

---

42 *Partisan Review* 23 (Fall, 1956), 568-573. Collected in Baldwin's *Nobody Knows My Name* (New York, 1961), pp. 117-126.

43 Page 7.

44 Pages 18-20.

45 See *The Reporter* 14 (Apr. 19, 1956), 5. Faulkner refers to himself as a "liberal" twice in *The Reporter* version. This section was left out of the text appearing in the *Sunday Times*.

46 Later in the same year Faulkner explained what he meant by the middle road. In *A Letter to the North* (*Life*, Mar. 5, 1956, pp. 51-52) he said that a small minority of white Southerners had remained apart from the general majority Southern point of view. They were "present yet detached, committed and attainted neither by citizens' council nor NAACP"; they were in "the middle,"

be on it. But if it came to fighting I'd fight for Mississippi against the United States even it it meant going out into the street and shooting Negroes. After all, I'm not going out to shoot Mississippians. (*the Reporter*, p. 19)

When Howe asked if he did not mean "white Mississippians," Faulkner replied "No, I said Mississippians—in Mississippi the problem isn't racial. Ninety per cent of the Negroes are on one side with the whites, against a handful like me who believe that equality is important." Later in the interview Faulkner apparently attempted to clarify what he meant by this statement when he said:

I will go on saying that the Southerners are wrong and that their position is untenable, but if I have to make the same choice Robert E. Lee made then I'll make it. My grandfather had slaves and he must have known that it was wrong, but he fought in one of the first regiments raised by the Confederate Army, not in defense of his ethical position but to protect his native land from being invaded. *(Ibid.)*

Despite this explanation and also the constant reiteration that the Negro has a right to equality, Faulkner's remark about "shooting Negroes" rankled many readers. That his detractors should fix on this remark, perhaps said in haste, and certainly misleading when taken out of context, is ironic; at one point in the interview Faulkner had insisted, "The Negroes are right —make sure you've got that—they're right."[47] Faulkner was later quite concerned about the furor his statement had made; indeed in a letter to the editor of *The Reporter*[48] he denied having made such statements:

but always drawn by "the simple human instinct to champion the underdog." "But where will we go," asks Faulkner, "if that middle becomes untenable? . . . If we, the (comparative) handful of Southerners . . . are compelled by the simple threat of being trampled if we don't get out of the way, to vacate that middle where we could have worked to help the Negro improve his condition—compelled to move for the reason that no middle any longer exists—we will have to make a new choice. And this time the underdog will not be the Negro, since he, the Negro, will be a segment of the topdog, and so the underdog will be that white embattled minority who are our blood and kin."

[47] This statement appears in the version of the interview printed in *The Reporter*; it is omitted from the text in the *Sunday Times*.

[48] *The Reporter*, Apr. 19, 1956, p. 19.

To the Editor: From letters I have received, and from quotations from it I have seen in *Time* and *Newsweek,* I think that some parts of the interview with me which I gave to the London *Sunday Times* interviewer and which, after notifying me, he made available to you, are not correct; needless to say, I did not read the interview before it went to print, nor have I seen it yet as printed.

If I had seen it before it went to print, these statements, which are not correct, could never have been imputed to me. They are statements which no sober man would make, nor, it seems to me, any sane man believe.

The South is not armed to resist the United States that I know of,[49] because the United States is neither going to force the South nor permit the South to resist or secede either.

The statement that I or anyone else would choose any one state against the whole remaining Union of States, down to the ultimate price of shooting other human beings in the streets, is not only foolish but dangerous. Foolish because no sane man is going to choose one state against the Union today. A hundred years ago, yes. But not in 1956. And dangerous because the idea can further inflame those few people in the South who might still believe such a situation possible.

Directly below Faulkner's letter was printed a statement by Russell Warren Howe:

All the statements attributed to Mr. Faulkner were directly transcribed by me from verbatim shorthand notes of the interview. If the more Dixiecrat remarks misconstrue his thoughts, I, as an admirer of Mr. Faulkner's, am glad to know it. But what I set down is what he said.

In a letter to *Time*[50] Faulkner repeated his repudiation of certain statements in the Howe interview:

---

49 Faulkner is referring to the statement attributed to him in the Howe interview: "The South is armed for revolt. After the Supreme Court decision [of May 17, 1954, on school integration] you couldn't get as much as a few rounds for a deer rifle in Mississippi. The gunsmiths were sold out. These white people will accept another Civil War knowing they're going to lose . . . . I know people who've never fired a gun in their lives but who've bought rifles and ammunition."

50 *Time,* Apr. 23, 1956, p. 12.

Sir: In our troubled times over segregation, it is imperative that no man be saddled with opinions on the subject which he has never held and, for that reason, never expressed. In New York last month . . . I gave an interview to a representative of the London *Sunday Times*, who (with my agreement) passed it on to the *Reporter*. I did not see the interview before it went into print. If I had, quotations from it which appeared in *Time*[51] could never have been imputed to me, since they contain opinions which I have never held, and statements which no sober man would make and, it seems to me, no sane man believe. That statement that I or anyone else in his right mind would choose any one state against the whole remaining Union of States, down to the ultimate price of shooting other human beings in the streets, is not only foolish but dangerous. Foolish, because no sane man is going to make that choice today even if he had the chance. A hundred years ago, yes, but not in 1956. And dangerous, because the idea can further inflame those few people in the South who might still believe such a situation possible.

The editor of *Time* printed the letter with a one sentence reply from Russell Howe: "If Mr. Faulkner no longer agrees with the more Dixiecratic of his statements I, for one, am very glad, but that is what he said."

Faulkner continued to deny having made the statements, and Howe politely but adamantly affirmed that he did. No new light was shed on the controversy until nine years later, when Horace Judson's article, "The Curse and the Hope," appeared in *Time* magazine.[52] Referring to the controversy, Judson said

---

[51] Faulkner refers to quotations from the Howe interview that appeared in the March 26 *Time* article on Mississippi Senator James O. Eastland ("The Authentic Voice," p. 26). The reference to Faulkner is: "Even 'moderate' Southerners for whom segregation was an indefensible evil are warning the North to keep hands off. Mississippi's Nobel Prizewinner William Faulkner, whose novels eloquently express the thoughtful Southerner's sense of moral guilt toward the Negro, recently told a British newspaperman: 'I don't like enforced integration any more than enforced segregation. If I have to choose between the United States Government and Mississippi, then I'll choose Mississippi against the United States, even if it meant going out into the street and shooting Negroes.' "

[52] *Time*, July 17, 1964, pp. 44-48.

Faulkner himself followed up the headlines with letters to many newspapers insisting that he had been misquoted by Howe. What the letters naturally did not mention was the fact that at the time of the interview Faulkner had spent several days working his way through a demijohn of bourbon, a bout set off by a running quarrel about the racial question with his brother John Faulkner, who was a die-hard segregationist.

Judson's explanation was quite intriguing, for in the letters to *The Reporter* and to *Time* Faulkner had said that "no sober man" would have made such statements. I queried Mr. Howe about the interview, particularly in regard to the remarks made by Horace Judson. Mr. Howe was most helpful in his reply and offered to supply me with a copy of his original question-and-answer notes taken during the interview. In a letter to me, dated March 7, 1965, Howe wrote:

> I expect you know that, because of the storm that the interview raised at the time, Faulkner later withdrew some of his franker statements, which he was widely quoted as saying were remarks that "no sober man would make and no sane man believe." About two weeks after the interview, Faulkner went into the hospital in Memphis, and *Time* Magazine passed on to me a remark he made to the magazine's string correspondent there: "I'd been drinking so much that week I might have said anything, and so much since I don't remember what I said." I should add that Faulkner gave no impression of inebriation: he was slow-spoken as usual, but didn't slur, misconstruct sentences or do anything else associated with people who are drunk. He chose the time and place of appointment himself (Scribner's office)[53] and confirmed it a few hours before, so presumably felt himself in a fit state to be interviewed. I sat about three or four feet from him the whole time, and caught no odor of bourbon.

---

[53] Howe is probably incorrect about Faulkner's choosing the Scribner office. Faulkner's biographer, Joseph Blotner, told me that he does not believe that Faulkner had any friends or acquaintances at Scribner's, and that the logical choices would have been Saxe Commins' office at Random House or Harold Ober's office.

Why he was so appallingly, even outrageously honest, I don't know; I guess he was just an honest person.

In a second letter dated March 23, 1965, Howe wrote:

I, also, think the in vino veritas implications, if justified, are interesting. Either he was not drunk, but felt he had gone too far, and so mistakenly thought that claiming to have been intoxicated at the time would imply that he had said things which he did not feel; or, of course, he was drunk, and I was too unfamiliar with Faulkner to recognize it—in which case he was speaking more uninhibitedly, frankly and truthfully than he would normally do when talking for publication.

Since Howe obviously doubted that Faulkner was inebriated at the time of the interview, I asked Horace Judson to give me details regarding his source of information. In a letter to me dated 20 September 1965, Judson replied:

I am sorry that I am not going to be able to be of much help on the question you raise. The fact that Faulkner had been drinking heavily at the time of that famous interview was told to us independently by at least two sources, both of whom had known Faulkner and the family. One of those sources also supplied the cause of the drinking bout, in the quarrel about race that Faulkner had been having with his brother. Both of our sources were reliable informants in the academic and publishing worlds. But both of them were talking to *Time* strictly "not for attribution"—which means, I am afraid, that I have personally promised not to reveal their identities. You will appreciate that this kind of pledge is sometimes necessary in journalism—and even in scholarly research when it approaches contemporary biography. I hope you will also appreciate that I have a deep regard for Faulkner and for Faulkner scholarship, and that therefore I greatly regret that I cannot further your research.

Doubtless Faulkner disagreed with the segregationist stand taken by his brother John, who in his biography, *My Brother Bill*, hints at a possible dissension over the race issue.

It was about this time that Bill started writing and talking integration. It did not set well with the rest of us but we felt toward him as he had toward Mother about her convalescence. We always felt that way toward each other when one of us did something contrary. If that's what he wants, let him alone.[54]

He added that none of the family "agreed with Bill's views" on integration, and that they were all relieved when he stopped writing "pro-integration" articles and speeches.[55] John Faulkner indicated, however, that Faulkner and he had settled their differences, and John Faulkner's widow denies that there was ever a "running quarrel" between her husband and William Faulkner. In a letter dated October 10, 1965, Mrs. John Faulkner told me that once "in a conversation" the subject of integration had come up. "Each [John and Bill] expressed his views and were in disagreement but there was no quarrel. Each one respected the other's opinion and it ended there."

Perhaps the real motivation for some of Faulkner's remarks during the interview will never be determined. Whether or not Faulkner was inebriated at the time he made the statements, he certainly wished to repudiate them later. In the interview itself there is abundant evidence to indicate that he was on the side of the Negro, and his article entitled "If I Were a Negro," which appeared in *Ebony* magazine[56] the following September, began with a repudiation of the statements concerning choosing Mississippi over the United States and shooting Negroes in the streets.

Faulkner's "Go Slow" Policy

Faulkner's "A Letter to the North" was published in the March 5, 1956, issue of *Life*, some two weeks before the considerably less temperate Howe interview appeared in *The Reporter*. By March, Faulkner had become quite alarmed over the continued eruption of violence resulting from the South's resistance to the integration of schools. Al-

---

54 John Faulkner, *My Brother Bill* (New York, 1963), p. 268.
55 *My Brother Bill*, p. 268.
56 *Ebony*, Sept., 1956, pp. 70-73.

ways in opposition to compulsory segregation, Faulkner nonetheless felt compelled to oppose compulsory integration and to warn the North and American liberals in general that to force integration upon the South would necessarily lead to mass bloodshed. He uses as an example the recent rioting at the University of Alabama caused by the admission of Autherine Lucy, a Negro. Faulkner quotes a New York *Times* editorial which said that the rioting was the first time that force and violence had become part of the integration question. But this is not true, says Faulkner, for to most Southerners (regardless of their stand on desegregation) the first promise of force and violence was the Supreme Court decision itself. He continues by citing instances of racial violence which occurred after the Court's ruling.

Faulkner is quite explicit in expressing his belief that the Northern liberal does not—and perhaps cannot—understand the South's sentiment regarding the racial situation. The problem is neither legal nor moral, but one of such emotional intensity that it could cause the South to go to any lengths and against any odds to defend its position. The North, says Faulkner, should have learned from the Civil War that the South will knowingly pursue a fatal course before it will accept alteration of its racial condition because of a legal or economic threat. Faulkner contends that many Southerners recognized the moral implications of the Civil War, but chose to fight for their own "blood and kin and home"; similarly, the comparatively few contemporary Southerners who, at the price of contumely and insult, have maintained a middle-of-the-road position between the two extremes of the white Citizens' Council and the NAACP, might find this position untenable should the same emotional reasons arise. Because of this, Faulkner urges all those who would compel immediate and unconditional integration to "go slow," to give the Southerner time to see that "nobody is going to force integration on him from the outside," and that he himself must rid his own land of a moral and physical condition which must be cured if he is ever to have any peace.

Faulkner's advice to "go slow" in his "A Letter to the North" caused immediate criticism. In his essay "Faulkner and Desegregation," published in the Fall 1956 issue of *Partisan Review* (p. 568-573), James Baldwin attacked Faulkner for his "middle-of-the-road" policy. On March 22 at the National Civil Liberties Union Clearing House, Dr. Carl R. Pritchett, a Presbyterian minister, Clarence Mitchell, representing the NAACP, and Dr. Frederick Routh, representing the Southern Regional Council, discussed the views Faulkner had expressed in the *Life* article and in the interview with Howe. The Clearing House, which included representatives from various national church, civic, and other groups, was sponsoring a conference on civil liberties in Washington, D.C.

Because of such criticism, Faulkner wrote a letter published in the March 26 issue of *Life* (p. 19) explaining his position in the article of March 5. Faulkner writes that since the publication of his "Letter to the North" he has received many replies from outside the South. Although many of the correspondents criticized the reasoning in Faulkner's essay, none of them seemed to understand the reasons behind it, a fact which indicates to Faulkner that he was correct in saying that non-Southerners cannot understand the South. Faulkner explains that his motivation for writing the letter was to save the nation from the blot of Autherine Lucy's death. Miss Lucy had just been suspended from the University of Alabama, and he had felt that when the judge abrogated the suspension, the forces supporting her enrollment at the University would send her back. Faulkner believed that if they did, Autherine Lucy would possibly lose her life. Since she was not sent back, the letter was not needed for that purpose, but Faulkner hopes that the letter may still serve to prevent the potential for such tragedy from arising again.

On April 15, at Oakland, California, Dr. W. E. B. Dubois, the eighty-eight-year-old co-founder of the NAACP, challenged Faulkner to a debate on integration. The challenge was issued in an interview recorded for Station KROW. The subject of the debate was to be the "go slow now" advice to Negroes in the March 5 *Life* article. Dubois suggested that the debate should take place on the court house steps at Sumner, Mississippi, where the Emmett Till murder case was tried. In a special report to the New York *Times*, dated San Francisco,

April 17, Faulkner's telegraphed reply was quoted: "I do not believe there is a debatable point between us. We both agree in advance that the position you will take is right morally, legally, and ethically. (If it is not evident to you) that the position I take in asking for moderation and patience is right practically, then we will both waste our breath in debate."

Faulkner's "go slow" advice in "A Letter to the North" and in his letter to the editor of *Life* (March 26) echoes sentiments he expressed in Japan in 1955. In a Press Club interview, Faulkner was asked if the living conditions of the Negro had recently improved. He replied:

> Yes, they have improved quite a lot. Not as much as they should, but they have improved a great deal, quite a lot. I think if the Negro himself has enough sense, tolerance, wisdom, to be still for a short time, there will be a complete equality in America. His black skin will make no difference. But he's the one that has got to be quiet and calm and intelligent, not the white man, because the white man is afraid that if the Negro has any social advancement his economic status will change. (*Faulkner at Nagano*, p. 5)

Asked about his opinion concerning the Supreme Court's decision on segregation in schools, Faulkner said that "it's right, it's just," but that the enforcement of the decision would be a problem. The enforcement will take time, and that, said Faulkner, is what he meant when he said that the Negro must be "patient and sensible."

While participating in the Summer Seminar in American Literature at Nagano, Japan (1955), Faulkner read an unpublished essay which he indicated would become a chapter in a book entitled *The American Dream (Faulkner at Nagano*, p. 96). Although the essay is not printed in *Faulkner at Nagano*, it is apparent that what Faulkner read at this session was the essay later printed in the June 1956 issue of *Harper's Magazine* as "On Fear: The South in Labor." Actually, this essay contains many paragraphs that are either literal transcriptions or else slightly altered versions of statements made by Faulkner in his address at the meeting of the Southern Historical

Association in Memphis, Tennessee, on November 10, 1955.

As Faulkner had indicated in his introductory remarks at Nagano, the essay deals not so much with racial discrimination as with "a choice that people must make between freedom and not being free." In the opening paragraph of the essay, Faulkner quotes his letter concerning the Mississippi public schools which had appeared in the March 20, 1955, Memphis *Commercial Appeal*, and goes on to allude to the many protests this letter provoked. Such protests are provoked, says Faulkner, by fear, a fear that can drive otherwise rational, cultured, and generous white Southerners to use contumely, threat, and insult as weapons against such views as his own which suggest that the betterment of the Negro's condition does not necessarily presage the doom of the white race.

The fear which Faulkner describes is not so much a fear of the Negro as an individual or a race but as an economic factor which threatens the economic system rather than the social system of the white man. Faulkner says that the white man dares not admit what he knows to be true; that because this economic system is established on an obsolescence (the artificial inequality of man) it is doomed. Faulkner cites the notable advances the American Negro has made from his naked ancestors in African rain forests and the slaves of the ante-bellum South. It is this record of achievement that instills the fear in the white Southerner; since the Negro has accomplished "so much with no chance," might he not accomplish even more with an equal chance, might he not "take the white man's economy away from him, the Negro now the banker or the merchant or the planter and the white man the sharecropper or the tenant?"

It is fear, says Faulkner, that drove the murderers of Emmett Till to kill a harmless child. In the Till incident, two adults kidnapped a fourteen-year-old boy in order to frighten him. However, the boy not only refused to be frightened but, alone and unarmed in the dark, he so frightened the two armed adults that they had to destroy him. It might be argued that Faulkner cannot logically use the Till murder as an example of the economic fear that he describes in his essay, for the fear which motivated the murderers of the young Negro was not economic in its origin, but sprang from the old obsession with the sexuality of the black man and with the purity of the white woman. Faulkner, however, would contend that even behind this fear is to be found the economic factor. "It is our Southern white man's shame," says Faulkner, "that in our present economy the Negro must not have economic equality; our double shame that we fear that giving him more social equality will jeopardize his present economic status; our triple shame that even then, to justify our stand, we must becloud the issue with the bugaboo of miscegenation." (*Harper's*, p. 34)

The above is almost a literal quotation of the statement Faulkner had made in his address to the Southern Historical Association, as are his statements about the necessity to "confederate, and confederate fast"—not as black or white people, but as people who are still free. Faulkner's metaphor of "homogeny" is recurrent in both the address and the essay.

Faulkner's next published statement on the racial question appeared in *Ebony* magazine in September 1956 (pp. 70-73). Entitled "If I Were a Negro," this essay begins with another refutation of his alleged statement about "shooting Negroes in the streets" and another attempt to elucidate precisely what he had meant in his "go slow" advice in the *Life* essay the previous March. Faulkner then proceeds to outline a course of action which he would follow were he a Negro. He would, he says, be a member of the NAACP, "since nothing else in our U.S. culture has yet held out to my race that much of hope," but he would remain in this organization only so long as it pursued a course of "inflexible and unviolent flexibility." Faulkner advises that the Negro should follow the path blazed by Gandhi and be certain that "if violence and unreason come, it must not come from us." In the *Life* article, Faulkner had advised the NAACP, the Northern liberal, and the federal government to go slow. Were he a Negro, says Faulkner, he would offer the same advice to his fellow Negroes: "I would say that our race must adjust itself psychologically, not to an indefinite continuation of a segregated society, but rather to a continuation as long as necessary of that inflexible unflagging flexibility which in the end will make the white man himself sick and tired of fighting it." The white man, says Faulkner, has spent three hundred years in teaching the Negroes to be patient, and, as a consequence, patience is the one thing in which the Negroes are the white man's superiors.

The implication of the final three paragraphs of "If I Were a Negro" is that the Negro is perhaps not quite ready for the responsibility of equality—an implication that is absent in earlier statements made by Faulkner. Still speaking in the role of a Negro, Faulkner says:

> We must learn to deserve equality so that we can hold and keep it after we get it. We must learn responsibility, the responsibility of equality. We must learn that there is no such thing as a "right" without any ties to it, since anything given to one free for nothing is worth exactly that: nothing. We must learn that our inalienable right to equality, to freedom and liberty and the pursuit of happiness, means exactly what our founding fathers meant by it: the right to *opportunity* to be free and equal, provided one is worthy of it, will work to gain it and then work to keep it. And not only the right to that opportunity, but the willingness and the capacity to accept the responsibility of that opportunity— the responsibilities of physical cleanliness and of moral rectitude, of a conscience capable of choosing between right and wrong and a will capable of obeying it, of reliability toward other men, the pride of independence of charity or relief.

The possibility that the Negro is not yet ready for total equality is again reiterated two years later in "A Word to Virginians," which Faulkner read at a meeting of the Raven, Jefferson, and ODK societies on February 20, 1958, at the University of Virginia.[57] In this address, Faulkner said "perhaps the Negro is not yet capable of more than second class citizenship. His tragedy may be that so far he is competent for equality only in ratio of his white blood" (p. 210); and again, "For the sake of argument, let us agree that as yet the Negro is incapable of equality for the reason that he could not hold and keep it even if it were forced on him with bayonets; that once the bayonets were removed, the first smart and ruthless man black or white who came along would take it away from him

---

57 *Faulkner in the University*, pp. 209-227.

because he, the Negro, is not yet capable of, or refuses to accept the responsbilities of equality" (p. 210). Nevertheless, Faulkner argues in his opening paragraph that no nation can long endure with ten per cent of its population unassimilated and forming a second-class citizenship because of the accident of its physical appearance. Thus, even if the Negro is not yet capable of more than second-class citizenship, or even if he is content to remain in such a position, the problem remains for the responsible (i.e., first class) citizens to solve. The white man, says Faulkner, must teach the Negro to be responsible, and he must teach him that in order to be free and equal, the Negro "must first be worthy of it, and then forever afterward work hard to hold and defend it." Faulkner feels that the responsibility for educating the Negro to his new role must be assumed by Southerners, for while the Southerner may never succeed in really knowing the Negro, at least he understands him better than the Northerner. The white man can never really know the Negro race because he has always forced the Negro to be a Negro rather than just another human being. Preparatory to assuming full equality in a free society, the Negro must "learn to cease forever more thinking like a Negro and acting like a Negro." This will not be an easy task, and it shall be the duty of the white citizens to educate the Negroes so that they will be capable of shouldering the burden of this new responsibility.

Faulkner's continuous reiteration of this sentiment in his later statements on the race question indicates another reason for his insistence on a "go slow" policy in integration: a too rapid alteration in the status quo would not only push an emotional segment of Southern society into open violence, but it would also prematurely push the Negroes into a role for which they are as yet unprepared and, until further education, incapable of assuming. Faulkner's main intention in this particular statement is to motivate Virginians to lead the rest of the South in educating the Negro for his new place in society. "So let it begin in Virginia," he says, "toward whom the rest of us are already looking as the child looks toward the parent for a sign, a signal where to go and how to go."

The NAACP's insistence on a rapid change of existing race

relations ultimately caused Faulkner's opposition to that organization. In the *Ebony* article of 1956 Faulkner had said that were he a Negro he would be a member of the NAACP, but only as long as that organization remained "flexible," that is, adaptable to circumstances and locality in its methods of gaining equality. By February of 1960, however, he is declining to contribute to the NAACP. Faulkner explains his attitude in a letter to his former Negro servant, Paul Pollard, who had written to him requesting money for the NAACP.[58]

I cannot send you this money. I will try to explain why. In the past I contributed indirectly to your organisation, since I believed it was the only organisation which offered your people any hope. But recently it has seemed to me that the orginastion [*sic*] is making mistakes. Whether it instigates them, or merely condones or takes advantage of them, it is anyway on the side of, in favor of, actions which will do your people harm, by building up to a situation where the white people who hate and grieve over the injustice which your people have to suffer, will be forced to choose either for or against their own people, and they too, the ones which your people consider the best among my people, will have to choose the side of the rest of the white people.

I agree with your own two great men: Booker T. Washington, and Dr. Carver. Any social justice and equality which is compelled to your people by nothing but law and police force, will vanish as soon as the police force is removed, unless the individual members of your race have earned the right to it . . . . Your people must earn by being individually responsible to bear it, the freedom and euqlity [*sic*] they want and should have. As Dr. Carver said, "We must make the white people need us, want us to be in equality with them."

I think your organisation is not doing that. Years ago, I set aside a fund of money which I am using, and will continue to use, in education, to teach the people of your race to *earn*

[58] This letter is reproduced in part in *Charles Hamilton Auction Catalog No. 21* (New York, 1967), pp. 72-73.

the right to equality, and to show the white people that they are and will be responsible to keep it. In Dr. Carver's words, *make, compel,* the white people to *want* them equal, not just to accept them in equality because police or military bayonets compel them to . . . .

. . . If the people of your race are to have equality and justice as human beings in our culture, the majority of them have got to be changed completely from the way they now act. Since they are a minority, they must behave better than white people. They must be *more* responsible, more honest, more moral, more industrious, more literate and educated. They, not the law, have got to compel the white people to say, Please come and be equal with us. If the individual Negro does not do this by getting himself educated and trained in responsibility and morality, there will be more and more trouble betwen [*sic*] the two races.

That is what I am using my money for, in individual cases . . . .

This personal letter to Pollard is Faulkner's last known utterance on the race question. Throughout his writing career, Faulkner exhibits an increasing concern with the Negro. In his fiction, the treatment of the Negro as an individual ends with the publication of *Intruder in the Dust,* for as Irving Howe points out, the Negro in *Requiem for a Nun* becomes a force for the salvation of the whites. In the twelve years following the publication of *Intruder in the Dust,* however, Faulkner made many nonfiction statements about the Negro question. Reaction against Faulkner's earlier statements came primarily from "conservatives" and from outright racists. The majority of these early statements are letters to the Memphis *Commercial Appeal* (1950-1955) and contain Faulkner's criticism of the segregated school system of Mississippi and the injustices received by Negroes in Southern courts.

In 1955, in his address to the Southern Historical Association and in the many comments he made on race in Japan, Faulkner continues to stress the economic basis for racial prejudice and to insist on the Negro's right to equality. In his remarks at the Nagano colloquies, however, Faulkner becomes more explicit in his assertions that equality for the Negro will be a slow process.

The year 1956 marks a change in emphasis in Faulkner's remarks on race. In the Howe interview, and in the essays in *Life* and *Ebony* magazines, Faulkner states his opposition to compulsory integration and urges a "go slow" policy in the implementation of the civil rights program. Several of his statements in 1956 take the tone of a warning against the North, and for the first time Faulkner begins to receive attacks from "liberals" and from Negroes who advocate the use of legal, and, if necessary, physical force to implement immediate and extensive enforcement of civil rights. Faulkner's "I'd fight for Mississippi" remark to Howe caused many to conclude that despite his sympathetic treatment of Negroes in his fiction, Faulkner was at heart just another old-guard Southerner. This opinion persisted even after Faulkner's repeated attempts to deny some of the statements attributed to him by Howe.

Faulkner and States' Rights

A 1957 letter to the editor of the Memphis *Commercial Appeal* indicates Faulkner's increasingly ambivalent feelings about civil rights versus states' rights.[59] In this letter, Faulkner expresses relief that the Eisenhower administration's civil rights bill was not passed. "A few years ago," writes Faulkner, "the Supreme Court rendered an opinion which we white Southerners didn't like, and we resisted it." According to Faulkner, the 1957 civil rights bill contained "a good deal more danger to us all than the presence of Negro children in white schools or Negro votes in white ballot boxes," yet, apparently, only an "expert" could see this danger. Similar bills will continue to be offered to Congress, says Faulkner, as long as Southerners continue to give the Negro only second-class citizenship in which he is "subject to taxation and military service, yet denied the political right to vote for, and the economic and educational competence to be represented among

[59] Memphis *Commercial Appeal*, Sept. 15, 1957.

those who tax and draft him." Ultimately, conjectures Faulkner, one of these bills will pass, for the "expert won't be there in time."

Faulkner does not state who the expert is who recognized the danger in the 1957 bill, but probably he is alluding to Georgia Senator Richard B. Russell. Some discussion of the bill's history should indicate Faulkner's fear of it in its original form and also explain his relief that the bill did not pass.

The Eisenhower administration's civil rights bill of 1957 was the result of three years of study by the United States Department of Justice under Attorney General Herbert Brownell, Jr. Although the United States had criminal statutes providing fines up to $5,000 and imprisonment of up to ten years for persons acting to deprive others of equal protection under the law (which included the right to vote in federal elections), the laws were generally ineffective because Southern juries would not vote for conviction. And although the United States had civil statutes under which a private citizen could file suit to protect his own civil rights, these also were frequently ineffective because of the time-consuming, expensive machinery of local administrative agencies and state courts which the litigant had to go through before he could take his case to the federal courts. The 1957 civil rights bill provided that a civil rights plaintiff would bypass the administrative agencies and state courts and take his case directly to the federal courts. The bill also provided for a new Assistant Attorney General to handle civil rights cases and set up a six-member bipartisan commission with subpoena powers to conduct a two-year study of civil rights. The most controversial provision contained in the bill, however, was the power given the United States Attorney General to file civil suits whenever any persons "have engaged" or when there are reasonable grounds to believe that any persons "are about to engage" in acts that would violate civil rights statutes.

On July 3, 1957, Senator Richard B. Russell called his Southern colleagues to a caucus in his office. Russell had participated in ten extended battles over race legislation during his twenty-four years in the Senate. In every instance the legislation had been withdrawn. This time, however, Russell pointed out that the tactics which had worked in the past (the Southern filibuster) might not work again. *Time* pointed out that the Solid South was decreasing in strength: Tennessee and Texas no longer attended Southern caucuses regularly, and "senatorial dependables" were down from twenty-two to eighteen.[60] Furthermore, they could no longer count on substantial aid or even neutrality from conservative Republicans who in the past had helped Southern Democrats to defeat the civil rights legislation of a Democratic administration. This time the bill had been proposed by President Eisenhower; Republican Senate Leader William F. Knowland was actively engaged in steering the legislation through the Senate; and Vice-President Richard Nixon was campaigning in the background. Instead of a preliminary filibuster, Russell suggested that the Southerners push for a drastic revision of the bill.

The Southern strategy was carefully plotted. Their case was built on an issue developed by North Carolina's Senator Sam Ervin, who had formerly served as judge on his state's Supreme Court. Ervin, a member of a judiciary subcommittee conducting hearings on the civil rights bill, began questioning the abolition of trial by jury. He argued that it would be a " 'tragic error to attempt the protection of civil rights for any one group through a process which denies a liberty equally precious—that of trial by jury.' "[61] He charged that the administration's civil rights proposals would do exactly that. In the caucus, Russell assigned the issue of "trial-by-jury," which became the Southerners' slogan, to Arkansas' William Fulbright (referred to in *Time* as "the darling of Northern literary liberals") and to Alabama's John Sparkman ("another man of liberal repute and Adlai Stevenson's running mate in 1952"). Alabama's Lister Hill ("a liberal in good standing with labor") was to sound the alarm among the ranks of organized labor (historically opposed to the use of federal court injunctions in strike situations), and Arkansas' John McClellan ("noted by television and general repute across the whole country for his stern morality") was to stress the "immorality"

---

60 "The Rearguard Commander," *Time* 70 (Aug. 12, 1957), 13-16.
61 "The Civil Rights Bill: What It Is and Where It Stands," *Time* 69 (May 6, 1957), 26.

of granting authority to the United States Attorney General to get injunctions from the federal courts to prevent abuses of all kinds of Negro rights. All were advised to take advantage of every opportunity to appear on radio and television programs such as "Meet the Press" and "Face the Nation."[62]

Russell assigned himself the job of delivering harsh words to the Senate. It was generally understood by the Southerners themselves that a diatribe from a Talmadge or an Eastland would predictably get lost, as usual, in the Senate whirl, but if it came from reasonable, respected Dick Russell, a sharp blast would be heard with respectful attention. Russell's warning about what would happen if the Senate passed the civil rights bill was widely reported in news magazines. *Time*, for example, in an article which featured Russell as the leader of the opposition to the bill, quoted the following statements from his address:

> If it is proposed to move into the South in this fashion, the concentration camps may as well be prepared now, because there will not be enough jails to hold the people of the South who will oppose the use of raw federal power forcibly to commingle white and Negro children in the same schools and in places of public entertainment.[63]

What Faulkner feared in the bill is indicated in another excerpt from Russell's address:

> The bill is cunningly designed to invest in the Attorney General unprecedented power to bring to bear the whole might of the Federal government, including the armed forces if necessary, to force a commingling of white and Negro children in the state-supported schools of the South. ... I speak in a spirit of great sadness. If Congress is driven to pass this bill in its present form, it will cause unspeakable confusion, bitterness, and bloodshed in a great section of our common country.[64]

---

[62] "The Rearguard Commander," *Time*, p. 14.
[63] *Ibid.*
[64] "Civil Rights—Best Chance?" *Newsweek* 50 (July 15, 1957), 23-24.

The strategy and the speech had exactly the effect Russell had intended. According to *Time,*

> President Eisenhower began to back away—"I was reading part of the bill this morning and there were certain phrases I didn't completely understand"—and set up a man-to-man meeting with Dick Russell in the White House. Such Northern Republicans as Massachusetts' Leverett Saltonstall and New Jersey's Alexander Smith, such Western liberal Democrats as Montana's Mike Mansfield and New Mexico's Clinton P. Anderson allowed that they had no notions of coercing the South. Such powerful Northern newspapers as the New York *Times,* Washington *Post* and *Times Herald* and the Washington *Star* carefully re-examining their consciences to see whether they were being fair to Russell's position, came out extolling a great many of its merits.[65]

Led by Russell and Senate Majority Leader Lyndon B. Johnson of Texas, Southerners managed to repeal a Reconstruction law that gave a President the authority to use federal troops to enforce civil rights laws. They also eliminated from the administration's bill the part authorizing the United States Attorney General to seek federal injunctions to prevent not only violations of voting rights, but also violations of other federally guaranteed civil rights, such as education in integrated schools. With this accomplished, the Southerners focused their assault on the jury trial issue. What they wanted was to write a provision into the bill which would provide jury trials, in some cases, for those accused of defying federal injunctions barring them from interfering with voting rights.

Republican Senator Knowland was confident he had the necessary votes—those of thirty-nine Republicans and ten Democrats—to defeat the amendment, but Johnson and his Southern forces managed to split the labor opposition to a jury-trial amendment and then use the new followers in labor to split the ranks of liberal Northern Democrats and Republicans. In place of a pending amendment by Wyoming Democrat Joseph C. O'Mahoney, which would have guaranteed jury trials

---

[65] "The Rearguard Commander," *Time,* p. 14.

in criminal contempt cases arising from the denial of voting rights, Johnson suggested that the jury guarantee be extended to all kinds of criminal contempt cases, including labor disputes and strikes. Johnson's amendment was met with approval from George Meany, president of the AFL-CIO, but with disapproval from Walter Reuther and James B. Carey, vice-presidents of the organization. Senator Richard Neuberger of Oregon, a liberal Democrat, had prepared an amendment of his own which he planned to offer only if the O'Mahoney amendment went through. Neuberger's amendment would have denied jury trials in states where jurors were selected only from the lists of registered voters, since this was an effective way to keep Negroes off jury panels. Johnson then asked Senator Frank Church of Idaho to propose Neuberger's amendment, in a somewhat modified form, as a revision of the O'Mahoney amendment.

The new amendment appealed to liberals, and after hours of pleading, Johnson persuaded Southerners to accept it. Under this proposal, white Southerners might have their jury trials, but Southern Negroes might be sitting on the jury. Civil contempt was used to force a defendant to comply with an order; criminal contempt was intended to punish past failure to comply. The line between the two could be a fine one; it would be up to the federal judge in each case to decide whether the action was criminal, therefore requiring a jury; or civil, with no jury.

After its passage by the Senate, the revised version of the civil rights bill went back to the House, where it was stalled for a week. House Democrats wanted to adopt the Senate version with one amendment: that the Senate provision requiring jury trials for all criminal contempt cases be narrowed to include only those pertaining to voting rights. House Republicans opposed the bill altogether on account of the jury-trial provision. House Republican Leader Joe Martin persuaded the four Republican members of the Rules Committee to hold out against the Senate bill and set New York's Republican Representative Kenneth Keating and Acting Attorney General Bill Rogers to work out a party position on the bill.

The proposal worked out by Keating and Rogers stipulated,

first, that the contempt-of-court provisions of the bill would apply to violations of voting rights only, and not to all criminal contempt cases, as the Senate bill provided; second, that in criminal contempt cases based on denial of the right to vote, federal judges would be allowed to set sentences of up to ninety days and fines of up to $300, but jury trials would be required for greater penalties.

After conferring secretly with Southern Senators, Johnson informed Sam Rayburn that the Senate would probably accept a sentence of thirty days and a fine of $200 as the dividing line between judicial decree and jury trials in criminal contempt cases having to do with voting rights. In a meeting with Senate leaders in Knowland's office, Johnson made his offer. Knowland held out for a sixty-day, $300 formula, and the meeting adjourned without agreement. Johnson made a telephone call to Eisenhower; shortly afterward, negotiating on the Senate floor, Knowland came down to forty-five days and Johnson raised the fine to $300.

The House passed the compromise version and sent it back to the Senate. In the Senate, Strom Thurmond of South Carolina made a last-minute move to have the bid sidetracked to the Judiciary Committee for further consideration, but the motion was defeated 66 to 18. Just before 9:00 o'clock that night, Thurmond, who, from the beginning, had favored filibuster over compromise, took the floor and talked for 24 hours and 18 minutes. Two hours after his filibuster had ended, the Senate passed the bill by a vote of 60 to 15.

A test of the federal government's power to enforce civil rights legislation came immediately after the passage of the extensively amended civil rights bill of 1957. The school desegregation crisis in Little Rock, Arkansas, erupted with violence and the use of federal troops in September 1957. The Little Rock crisis, and particularly President Eisenhower's decision to deploy federal troops, caused Faulkner to assume a more positive states' rights stand.

Faulkner, of course, never identifies with the Bilbo or Vardaman mentality—a mentality which he attacks both implicitly and explicitly in his fiction as well as his nonfiction. But if Faulkner has a deep-rooted love and respect for the Negro, his love for his region is perhaps even stronger. This fact, which is evident in the hyperbolic statements made to Howe and in the more restrained statements made elsewhere, accounts for the many contradictory, vague, or equivocal statements made after 1957. Faulkner's love for the South also accounts for his paradoxical stance in his letter attacking the Eisenhower administration's civil rights bill. By 1957, Faulkner finds himself in the anomalous position of believing in both civil rights and states' rights. The difficulty in maintaining this position is reflected in the contradictory or cryptic nature of many of his later statements concerning Negro equality. Faulkner had always wanted a steady but gradual change in the status of the Negro, but as the Negro's unwillingness to wait makes a gradual change impossible, Faulkner becomes more and more alarmed.

Faulkner consistently maintains that the race problem must be solved, but that a genuine and lasting equality for the Negro will require at least a half-century. What is needed, insists Faulkner, is a workable plan for the reeducation of both the white and black races while civil rights are being gradually granted to those Negroes who are prepared to accept the responsibilities attendant to equality. Faulkner is convinced that forceful integration will only create an atmosphere of hostility that will further estrange the two races.

It should be remembered that Faulkner is an artist who felt compelled by the existing crisis in race relations to assume the role of a polemicist, a role for which he was not technically trained. Although he has a genuine respect for the Negro, Faulkner never really professes to understand him. He does, however, understand the Southern white. What Faulkner proposes is an ideal—the harmony of mankind. Nevertheless, Faulkner's insights into the contemporary race question are quite perceptive, and the history of events since his death have shown that much of his advice and admonitions are uncannily prophetic; within three months after his death military vehicles were rolling across the campus of the University of Mississippi,[66] and within a few years the large cities of Los Angeles, Chicago, and Detroit were torn by racial strife.

Faulkner's nonfiction statements on racial equality represent the opinions of the greatest American writer of the twentieth century on the most crucial problem his country has ever faced. If some of these statements seem to be in conflict with Faulkner's treatment of the Negro in his fiction, it is because in his fiction Faulkner is suggesting the ideal, while in his nonfiction he is delineating the real. Faulkner realizes that, unfortunately, there is a vast difference between what should be and what is. As Faulkner says in the Howe interview, "The Negro has a right to equality. His equality is inevitable, an irresistible force, but as I see it you've got to take into consideration human nature which at times has nothing to do with moral truths. Truth says this and fact says that. A wise person says, 'Let's use this fact. Let's obliterate this fact first.' To oppose a physical fact with a moral truth is silly."

---

66 The campus of the University of Mississippi was the scene of much rioting after the admission of a Negro student. Among the federal and state troops dispatched to the university was Troop E of the Second Reconnaissance Squadron, 108th Armored Cavalry Division. This unit was commanded by William Faulkner's nephew, Captain Murry C. Falkner, who suffered two broken bones during the rioting. Before the riots were ended, approximately 16,000 soldiers were sent to Oxford, Mississippi, and its environs—more than the combined population of the town and its university. See *Time*, Oct. 12, 1962, pp. 19-22.

Bibliography

PRIMARY SOURCES

FAULKNER, WILLIAM

Absalom, Absalom! New York: Modern Library, 1951.

Collected Stories of William Faulkner, New York: Random House, 1950.

Go Down, Moses. New York: Modern Library, 1942.

The Hamlet. New York: Random House, 1940.

Intruder in the Dust. New York: Modern Library, 1948.

Light in August. New York: Modern Library, 1950.

The Unvanquished. New York: Random House, 1965.

FAULKNER, WILLIAM

"American Segregation and the World Crisis," in *The Segregation Decisions,* ed. Bell Wiley. Atlanta, 1956.

"If I Were A Negro," *Ebony* (Sept. 1956), 70-73.

Letter to the Editor, *Life* 40 (Mar. 26, 1956), 19.

Letter to the Editor, Memphis *Commercial Appeal,* Mar. 26, 1950, sec. IV, p. 4.

Letter to the Editor, Memphis *Commercial Appeal,* Apr. 9, 1950, sec. IV, p. 4.

Letter to the Editor, Memphis *Commercial Appeal,* Feb. 20, 1955, sec. V, p. 3.

Letter to the Editor, Memphis *Commercial Appeal,* Mar. 20, 1955, sec. V, p. 3.

Letter to the Editor, Memphis *Commercial Appeal,* Apr. 3, 1955, sec. V, p. 3.

Letter to the Editor, Memphis *Commercial Appeal,* Apr. 10, 1955, sec. V, p. 3.

Letter to the Editor, Memphis *Commercial Appeal,* Apr. 17, 1955, sec. V, p. 3.

Letter to the Editor, Memphis *Commercial Appeal,* Sept. 15, 1957, sec. V, p. 8.

Letter to the Editor, New York *Times,* Oct. 13, 1957, sec. IV, p. 10.

Letter to the Editor, *The Reporter* 14 (Apr. 19, 1956), 7.

Letter to the Editor, *Time* 67 (Apr. 23, 1956), 12.

Letter to Paul E. Pollard, partially reproduced in *Charles Hamilton Auction Catalogue No. 21.* New York, 1967.

"On Fear: The South in Labor," *Harper's* 212 (June, 1956), 29-34.

"On Privacy," *Harper's* 211 (July, 1955), 33-38.

Statement to the Press on the Emmett Till Case, New York *Herald-Tribune,* Sept. 9, 1955, p. 36.

Statement to the Press on the Willie McGee Case, Memphis *Commercial Appeal*, Mar. 27, 1951, p. 4.

Text of the Address to the Southern Historical Association, Memphis *Commercial Appeal*, Nov. 11, 1955, p. 8.

"A Word to Virginians," in *Faulkner in the University*, ed. Frederick L. Gwynn and Joseph L. Blotner. Charlottesville, 1959.

INTERVIEWS,
SEMINARS,
REMINISCENCES

FANT, JOSEPH L., AND ROBERT ASHLEY, EDS.
Faulkner at West Point. New York, 1964.

FAULKNER, JOHN
My Brother Bill. New York, 1963.

96

GWYNN, FREDRICK L., AND JOSEPH L. BLOTNER, EDS.
Faulkner in the University. Charlottesville, 1959.

HOWE, RUSSELL WARREN
"New Civil War If Negro Claims Are Pressed," London *Sunday Times*, Mar. 4, 1956, p. 7.

"A Talk With William Faulkner," *The Reporter* 14 (Mar. 20, 1956), 18-20.

JELLIFFE, ROBERT A.
Faulkner at Nagano. Tokyo, 1956.

RESPONSES TO FAULKNER'S STATEMENTS ON RACE

BALDWIN, JAMES
"Faulkner and Desegregation," *Partisan Review* 23 (Fall 1956), 568-573.

Nobody Knows My Name. New York, 1961.

BELL, CHARLES W.
Letter to the Editor, Memphis *Commercial Appeal*, Apr. 17, 1955, sec. V, p. 3.

BONGARTZ, ROY
"Give Them Time: Reflections on Faulkner," *Nation* 182 (Mar. 31, 1956), 259.

"Faulkner Bars Debate" (news release), New York *Times*, Apr. 18, 1956, p. 29, col. 1.

"Faulkner Challenged" (news release), New York *Times*, Apr. 16, 1956, p. 8, col. 7.

"Faulkner Disputed on Civil Rights View" (news release), New York *Times*, Mar. 23, 1956, p. 28, col. 8.

" 'Go Slow Now' " (editorial), *Life* 40 (Mar. 12, 1956), 37.

HOWE, RUSSELL WARREN
Statement on the Interview with Faulkner, *The Reporter* 14 (Apr. 19, 1956), 7.
Statement on the Interview with Faulkner, *Time* 67 (Apr. 23, 1956), 12.

JONES, BILLY
Letter to the Editor, Memphis *Commercial Appeal*, Apr. 24, 1955, sec. V, p. 3.

LITTLEJOHN, TALMADGE D.
Letter to the Editor, Memphis *Commercial Appeal*, Apr. 17, 1955, sec. V, p. 3.

MARTIN, C. J.
Letter to the Editor, Memphis *Commercial Appeal*, Mar. 27, 1955, sec. V, p. 3.

NEILL, W. C.
Letter to the Editor, Memphis *Commercial Appeal*, Mar. 27, 1955, sec. V, p. 3.
"The South: The Authentic Voice," *Time* 67 (Mar. 26, 1956), 26-29.

STEPHENS, CLAYTON
Letter to the Editor, Memphis *Commercial Appeal*, Apr. 2, 1950, sec. IV, p. 4.

STUDENT
Letter to the Editor, Memphis *Commercial Appeal*, Feb. 6, 1955, sec. V, p. 3.

WOLSTENHOLME, T. T.
Letter to the Editor, Memphis *Commercial Appeal*, Feb. 6, 1955, sec. V, p. 3.

WOMACK, DAVE
Letter to the Editor, Memphis *Commercial Appeal*, Mar. 27, 1955, sec. V, p. 3.
Letter to the Editor, Memphis *Commercial Appeal*, Apr. 10, 1955, sec. V, p. 3.
Letter to the Editor, Memphis *Commercial Appeal*, Apr. 24, 1955, sec. V, p. 3.

CRITICAL APPRAISAL OF FAULKNER'S STATEMENTS ON THE RACE QUESTION

BACKMAN, MELVIN
Faulkner: The Major Years. Bloomington, 1966.

CAMPBELL, HARRY M., AND RUEL E. FOSTER
William Faulkner: A Critical Appraisal. Norman, 1951.

EDMONDS, IRENE C.
"Faulkner and the Black Shadow," *Southern Renascence: The Literature of the Modern South.* Louis D. Rubin, Jr. and Robert D. Jacobs, eds. Baltimore, 1953. Pages 192-206.

FAULKNER, JOHN
My Brother Bill: An Affectionate Remembrance. New York, 1963.

GEISMAR, MAXWELL
"William Faulkner: The Negro and the Female," *Writers in Crisis.* Boston, 1942. Pages 143-148.

HOFFMAN, FREDRICK J.
"The Negro and the Folk," *William Faulkner.* New York, 1961. Pages 80-101.

HOWE, IRVING
William Faulkner: A Critical Appraisal. New York, 1952.

NILON, CHARLES H.
Faulkner and the Negro. ("University of Colorado Studies: Series in Language and Literature," No. 8). Boulder, 1962.

ARTICLES

CARTER, HODDING
"Faulkner and his Folk," *Princeton University Library Chronicle* 18 (Spring 1957), 95-107.

GILES, BARBARA
"The South of William Faulkner," *Masses and Mainstream* 3 (Feb. 1950), 26-40.

GLICKSBERG, CHARLES I.
"William Faulkner and the Negro Problem," *Phylon* 10 (Second Quarter, 1949), 153-160.

GLOSTER, HUGH M.
"Southern Justice," *Phylon* 10 (First Quarter, 1949), 93-95.

GREER, DOROTHY D.
"Dilsey and Lucas: Faulkner's Use of the Negro as a Gauge of Moral Character," *Emporia State Research Studies*, XI, i, 43-61.

HOWE, IRVING
"William Faulkner and the Negro: A Vision of Lost Fraternity," *Commentary* 12 (Oct. 1951), 359-368.

HOWE, RUSSELL WARREN
"A Talk with William Faulkner," *The Reporter* 14 (Mar. 22, 1956), 18-20.

HOWELL, ELMO
"A Note on Faulkner's Negro Characters," *The Mississippi Quarterly* 2 (Fall 1958), 201-203.

PEAVY, CHARLES D.
"Faulkner and the Howe Interview," *College Language Association Journal* 11 (Dec. 1967), 117-123.

SEIDEN, MELVIN
"Faulkner's Ambiguous Negro," *Massachusetts Review* 4 (Summer 1963), 675-690.

VIERTEL, TOM
"Mr. Faulkner's Position on Equality," *Coastlines* 5 (Summer 1956), 33-34.

WILSON, EDMUND
"The James Branch Cabell Case Re-opened," *The New Yorker* 32 (Apr. 21, 1956), 140-168.
"William Faulkner's Reply to the Civil Rights Program," *The New Yorker* 24 (Oct. 23, 1948), 120-122, 125-128.

DISSERTATIONS
AND THESES

BLISSARD, THOMASINA
"The Role of the Negro in William Faulkner's Yoknapatawpha Series." (Unpublished master's thesis, Vanderbilt University, 1948).

DOSTER, WILLIAM CLARK
"William Faulkner and the Negro." (Unpublished doctoral dissertation, University of Florida, 1955).

HIATT, DAVID F.
"William Faulkner and the Yoknapatawpha Negro." (Unpublished master's thesis, University of New Mexico, 1956).

MORELAND, AGNES LOUISE
"The Negro in the Fiction of William Faulkner." (Unpublished master's thesis, University of Washington, 1953).
"A Study of Faulkner's Presentation of Some Problems that Relate to Negroes." (Unpublished doctoral dissertation, Columbia University, 1960).

PLAYER, RALEIGH PRESTON, JR.
"The Negro Character in the Fiction of William Faulkner." (Unpublished doctoral dissertation, University of Michigan, 1965).

STEINBERG, AARON
  "William Faulkner and the Negro." (Unpublished doctoral dissertation, New York University, 1966).

TAYLOR, WALTER FULLER
  "The Roles of the Negro in William Faulkner's Fiction." (Unpublished doctoral dissertation, Emory University, 1964).

BACKGROUND MATERIAL

BOOKS

DOYLE, BERTRAM W.
  The Etiquette of Race Relations in the South. Chicago, 1937.

100

FRANKLIN, JOHN HOPE
  From Slavery to Freedom. New York, 1952.

MILLER, KENT S.
  "Psychological Characteristics of the Negro," *The Negro in American Society.* Tallahassee, 1958.

MYRDAL, GUNNAR
  An American Dilemma: The Negro Problem and Modern Democracy. New York, 1944.

WHARTON, VERNON L.
  The Negro in Mississippi, 1865-1890. The James Sprunt Studies in History and Political Science. Chapel Hill, 1947.

WILEY, BELL
  Southern Negroes, 1861-1865. New Haven, 1938.

NEWS ARTICLES

"The Accused"
  Newsweek 46 (Sept. 19, 1955), 38.
"Alabama's Scandal"
  Time 67 (Feb. 20, 1956), 40.
"Arkansas: Case No. 3113"
  Time 70 (Sept. 30, 1957), 17; 19.
"Around the Beat"
  Newsweek 47 (Mar. 26, 1956), 90-91.
"A Boy Goes Home"
  Newsweek 46 (Sept. 12, 1955), 32.
"Civil Fight on Civil Rights"
  Time 69 (June 17, 1957), 17.
"Civil Rights—Best Chance?"
  Newsweek 50 (July 15, 1957), 23-24.
"The Civil Rights Bill: What It Is & Where It Stands"
  Time 69 (May 6, 1957), 26.

"Civil-Rights Victory"
  Time 69 (June 24, 1957), 25-26.
"Compromised Compromise"
  Time 70 (Sept. 2, 1957), 13-14.
" 'The Dam Is Breaking' "
  Time 70 (Aug. 26, 1957), 12-13.
"Eisenhower: Faubus"
  U.S. News & World Report 42 (Sept. 13, 1957), 28.
"Emmett Till's Day in Court"
  Life 39 (October. 3, 1955), 36-38.
"The End of Willie McGee"
  Life 30 (May 21, 1951), 44.
"The Entry of Mississippi Hoodlums"
  Nation 171 (Aug. 5, 1950), 118-119
"Hillbilly Slightly Sophisticated"
  Time 70 (Sept. 16, 1957), 24.

HUIE, WILLIAM BRADFORD
  "Shocking Story of an Approved Killing in Mississippi," *Look* 20
(Jan. 24, 1956), 46-48, 50.
  "What's Happened to the Emmett Till Killers?" *Look* 21 (Jan. 22,
1957), 63-67.

JUDSON, HORACE
  "The Curse & The Hope," *Time* 84 (July 17, 1964), 44-48.

"Jury Trials and Contempt"
  Time 70 (Aug. 12, 1957), 12.
"Justice and the Communists"
  Time 57 (May 14, 1951), 26.
"The Last, Hoarse Gasp"
  Time 70 (Sept. 9, 1957), 23-24.
"Life for Three Deaths"
  Newsweek 35 (Apr. 3, 1950), 21-22.
"Making a Crisis in Arkansas"
  Time 70 (Sept. 16, 1957), 23-25.
"Mixed-School Issue Comes to a Head"
  U.S. News & World Report 43 (Sept. 13, 1957), 27-30.

MOORE, ELLIS
  "Eyes of the Nation on Mississippi Trial," Memphis *Commercial
Appeal*, Mar. 12, 1950, sec. II, p. 12.

MOSTERT, MARY
  "Death for Association," *Nation* 172 (May 5, 1951), 421.

"Now—Or Never?"
  Newsweek 50 (August 5, 1957), 24-25.

"Pains of History"
  Time 70 (Sept. 16, 1957), 23.
"The Place, the Acquittal"
  Newsweek 46 (Oct. 3, 1955), 24; 29-30.
" 'Quick, Hard & Decisive' "
  Time 70 (Oct. 7, 1957), 21-25.
"The Rearguard Commander"
  Time 70 (Aug. 12, 1957), 13-16.
"Retreat from Newport"
  Time 70 (Sept. 23, 1957), 11.
"A Round for the South"
  Time 70 (July 22, 1957), 12.
"Round Two in Alabama"
  Time 67 (Mar. 12, 1956), 12.
"Segregation Victory?"
  Newsweek 47 (Mar. 12, 1956), 38-40.
"A Stay for Willie"
  Newsweek 36 (Aug. 7, 1950), 31-32.
"Swift Southern Justice"
  Newsweek 35 (Mar. 27, 1950), 22.
"Third Force"
  Time 70 (Aug. 5, 1957), 9-10.
"Trial by Jury"
  Time 66 (Oct. 3, 1955), 18-19.
" 'Vicious Stuff' "
  Time 70 (July 29, 1957), 13.
"Violence in Alabama"
  (editorial), New York *Times*, Feb. 10, 1956, sec. I, p. 20, col. 2.

WAKEFIELD, DAN
  "Justice in Summer," *Nation* 181 (Oct. 1, 1955), 284-285.

"What Orval Hath Wrought"
  Time 70 (Sept. 23, 1957), 11-14.
"What's in the Works"
  Newsweek 50 (July 22, 1957), 22-23.
"The Windy Windup"
  Newsweek 50 (Sept. 9, 1957), 32.

PERSONAL
LETTERS

FAULKNER, MRS. JOHN
  Letter to Charles D. Peavy, dated Oct. 10, 1965.

HOWE, RUSSELL WARREN
  Typescript Letter to Charles D. Peavy, dated Mar. 7, 1965.
  Typescript Letter to Charles D. Peavy, dated Mar. 23, 1965.

JUDSON, HORACE
  Typescript Letter to Charles D. Peavy, dated Sept. 20, 1965.

Index

Backman, Melvin, 24-25, 27
Baldwin, James, 68-69, 77
Birney, Earle, 22
Boyle, Bertram W., 40-41
body servants, 26-27
Breit, Harvey, 12
Brumm, Ursala, 15
Bunker, Robert, 12

Cabell, James Branch, 48
Cable, George Washington, 39
caste and class among slaves, 16, 18-19
Civil Rights Bill of 1957, 85-91

Dollard, John, 39
DuBois, W. E. B., 43, 77
Dunbar, Paul Lawrence, 40-41

economic basis for racism, 19-21, 47, 61, 62, 78-80
Ellison, Ralph, 24, 25, 42-43
Emmett Till murder trial, 66-68

Faulkner at Nagano, 33, 47, 50, 61. 62, 78
Faulkner in the University, 16, 33, 60
Faulkner, John, 73, 74-75
Faulkner, Mrs. John, 75
Faulkner, William,
  General Topics:
  amalgamation of races seen as ultimate solution to race problem, 33; assumes states' rights stand, 91-92; attacked in the press for his stand on the race issue, 59-60; attitude that non-Southerners cannot understand the South, 77, 78; attitude toward NAACP, 83-84; body servants in fiction, 27; desegregation, 76-77; Emmett Till murder, 67-68, 79; expresses views on the Howe interview, 70-73; fictional treatment of poor whites, 18-19, 20-21; Gavin Stephens as spokesman for Faulkner, 46-49; "go slow" policy, 75-76, 78, 80-81; importance of education for blacks stressed, 64-65, 83-84; Little

Rock school crisis, 64-65; Faulkner's loyalty to South, 48-49; miscegenation, 32-37; natural antagonism between the races, 64-65; Negro's self-hatred portrayed, 44; racism, 37, 38, 44, 68; role playing of Negro, 39-40, 44-45; Southern law enforcement officers portrayed, 45-46; states' rights, 85-93; telegraphed reply to challenge of W. E. B. DuBois, 78; views on integration and segregation, 68-75; view that basis for contemporary racial strife essentially economic, 20-21, 47, 61-62, 78-80; Willie McGee trial, 53, 56.

  Characters:
  Henry Beauchamp, 15; Lucas Beauchamp, 39-40; Charles Bon, 32, 35, 36-37; Lucas Burch, 45-46; Burden family, 29-30; Joanna Burden, 38; Nathaniel Burden, 38; Joe Christmas, 37; Clytie, 32, 35; Goodhue Coldfield, 16; Rosa Coldfield, 15; Doom, 17-18; Roth Edmonds, 15; Elnora, 21, 35; Sam Fathers, 18, 39; Reverend Hightower, 16; Ikkemotubbe, 18; Issetibbeha, 17; Loosh, 22, 23, 24; Shreve (Shrevlin) McCannon, 32; Carothers McCaslin, 18, 36; Eunice McCaslin, 36; Ike McCaslin, 15, 36; Uncle Buck McCaslin, 16, 44; Uncle Buddy McCaslin, 16; Chick Mallison, 44, 50; Nancy, 44; Philadelphy, 27-28; Ringo, 23, 25, 27, 30-31, 37; Aleck Sander, 39; Bayard Sartoris, 22-23, 24, 25, 27, 30, 35, 46; Colonel John Sartoris, 31; John Sartoris, 29-30; Lump Snopes, 45; Mink Snopes, 45; Gavin Stephens, 16, 46-49, 53; Eulalia Sutpen, 35, 36; Henry Sutpen, 36; Judith Sutpen, 36; Thomas Sutpen, 18, 19, 35, 36; Three-Basket, 16, 17; Tomasina, 36; Tomey's Turl, 36; Wash Jones, 19; Saucier Weddell, 27.

103